"In *Harvesting Freedom*, Gabriel Allahdua powerfully tells his story, starting with his early years in St. Lucia, to his decision to seek greener pastures in Canada after a hurricane destroyed his livelihood, to the many excruciating years he worked as a migrant farm worker under the Seasonal ⸱ ⸱ ⸱ years as an activist wit ⸱ ⸱ ⸱ sworth convincingly ⸱ ⸱ ⸱ practi- ces of indentᵢ ⸱ ⸱ ⸱ today's exploitation o ⸱ ⸱ ⸱ l heart- felt, *Harvestin* ⸱ ⸱ ⸱

—**Ethel Tu** ⸱ ⸱ ⸱ gration
p ⸱ ⸱ ⸱ versity

"In this fascinating first-person account of the making of an activist in the migrant workers' justice movement, Gabriel Allahdua offers both a scathing indictment of the temporary farm labour system that initially brought him to Canada from St. Lucia and an empowering story of the collective struggle of all migrant workers for respect, dignity, and immigrant status on arrival."

> —**Franca Iacovetta**, professor emerita, University of Toronto

"An exposé of the practices on Canadian farms that even those who are aware of the migrant worker system will be moved by. Gabriel Allahdua is a superb commentator on the migrant worker's life because he lived it, analyzed it, and, with the activism this book describes, is helping to change it. An infuriating system has produced an inspiring whistle-blower."

> —**Karen Dubinsky**, professor of history and global development studies, Queen's University

"By tracing the story of a hurricane in St. Lucia that spurred Gabriel Allahdua's path from beekeeper and teacher to migrant farm worker and activist, this book provides the first published chronicle of the life of a migrant farm worker in Canada. *Harvesting Freedom* not only disrupts the dehumanization that's baked into Canada's Seasonal Agricultural Worker Program, but it also provides a galvanizing account of migrant workers' collective struggle for justice and dignity. Given the expansion of unfree migrant worker programs worldwide amid the climate crisis, this firsthand account from a migrant farm worker and organic intellectual is globally significant."

—**Anelyse M. Weiler**, assistant professor, University of Victoria

"*Harvesting Freedom* offers a compelling and unflinching portrayal of the deep injustices facing migrant farm workers in Canada. Far more than just the story of one migrant farmer worker, *Harvesting Freedom* connects deeply personal struggles with broader consequences of colonialism, imperialism, capitalism, and white supremacy. Whether you are familiar with the Seasonal Agricultural Worker Program or new to the structural oppression facing migrant farm workers, *Harvesting Freedom* offers valuable insight into the racist realities of Canada's immigration system, and the possibilities that emerge through solidarity, empowerment, and collective organizing."

—**Amanda Wilson**, assistant professor, School of Social Innovation, Saint Paul University

"This is a book that touches the reader's heart, soul, and conscience. Written with Edward Dunsworth, Gabriel Allahdua generously shares with us his journey through colonial and neocolonial exploitation, from genocide, slavery, displacement, and extractive capitalism in the Caribbean to the ongoing 'legal' exploitation of migrant workers in Canada. The energy and passion that transpire from these pages reflect awareness deeply rooted in personal lived experience; the courage to learn; and full commitment to radical active hope. Hope that migrant justice, and food justice, will become the new normal for future generations in Canada and beyond."

—**Andrea A. Cortinois**, assistant professor, University of Toronto

HARVESTING FREEDOM

The Life of a
Migrant Worker
in Canada

GABRIEL ALLAHDUA
with Edward Dunsworth

Between the Lines
Toronto

Harvesting Freedom
© 2023 Gabriel Allahdua

First published in 2023 by
Between the Lines
401 Richmond Street West, Studio 281
Toronto, Ontario · M5V 3A8 · Canada
1-800-718-7201 · www.btlbooks.com

Library and Archives Canada Cataloguing in Publication
Title: Harvesting freedom : the life of a migrant worker in Canada / by Gabriel
    Allahdua, with Edward Dunsworth.
Names: Allahdua, Gabriel, author. | Dunsworth, Edward, author.
Description: Includes bibliographical references and index.
Identifiers: Canadiana (print) 20220454078 | Canadiana (ebook) 20220454140 |
    ISBN 9781771136181 (softcover) | ISBN 9781771136198 (EPUB)
Subjects: LCSH: Allahdua, Gabriel. | LCSH: Agricultural laborers, Foreign—
    Canada—Biography. | LCSH: Foreign workers, West Indian—Canada—
    History. | LCGFT: Autobiographies.
Classification: LCC HD1529 .A45 2023 | DDC 331.5/44092—dc23

Cover design by Farrah Miranda
Text design by DEEVE

Printed in Canada

We acknowledge for their financial support of our publishing activities: the Government of Canada; the Canada Council for the Arts; and the Government of Ontario through the Ontario Arts Council, the Ontario Book Publishers Tax Credit program, and Ontario Creates.

CONTENTS

I AM MANY THINGS

I am many things in Canada . . .

a God
*for my surname, Allahdua, a Muslim name for God;
from my ancestor on my father's side, an indentured
worker from India*

an Angel
*for my given name, the Angel Gabriel; from Christianity,
a religion imposed on my ancestors: colonization;
they've made me an angel, because my labour is used to
create somebody else's heaven*

a Slave
*like my mother's ancestors, exploited for my labour, far
away from home*

a Half Human
*denied basic human rights; second-class under
Canadian law*

a Lab Rat
*in a grand employment experiment. Everything that is
being introduced into the Canadian workplace—short-
term, contract, "flexible" employment—has been tried
on us for fifty-seven years.*

**What they try on migrant farm workers, they'll try on
you next.**

PREFACE
Edward Dunsworth

This book tells the life story of Gabriel Allahdua, a migrant farm worker turned leading migrant justice activist, in his own words: from his childhood in his home country of St. Lucia, to his experiences in the Seasonal Agricultural Worker Program (SAWP), to his life, work, and advocacy since leaving the program and settling permanently in Canada.

This book is the product of a collaboration between Gabriel and me, a historian of labour and migration. In this preface, I outline the history of the SAWP, provide some context for Gabriel's story, and describe the method by which Gabriel and I produced this volume. Readers eager to dive into Gabriel's story should not be shy about skipping ahead to chapter one and coming back to the preface later.

Gabriel was born in 1971 in St. Lucia, a small island country located in the Eastern Caribbean. Originally peopled by seafaring paddlers from the south some four thousand or more years ago, St. Lucia was home to perhaps 150 generations of Indigenous peoples—with all the complex histories of culture, language, technology, religion, migration, and warfare that such a broad sweep of time entails—before Europeans first set foot upon the island, sometime in the sixteenth century. It was not until the 1630s, however, that serious efforts by Europeans to establish colonies began, undertaken by English and French colonists and frequently marked by violence perpetrated against the island's Kalinago inhabitants, who resisted these incursions. In 1650 a French colony was established, and over the next century and a half the island would pass back and forth repeatedly between British and French hands. As Gabriel put it to me, "We were seven times colonized by France and seven times by England." The European invaders rapidly decimated the island's Indigenous population—though it never disappeared entirely—and by the next century had established St. Lucia as a sugar-producing slave colony, importing thousands of enslaved Africans to perform the back-breaking labour of planting, tending, harvesting, and processing sugar cane. After the abolition of slavery by Great Britain in 1834, planters turned in part towards indentured labourers from India to produce the sugar crop.[1] As a descendant of both enslaved Africans (on his mother's side) and indentured Indians (on his father's), Gabriel's family history is deeply intertwined with St. Lucia's history of colonization and exploitation of unfree, imported labour.

Gabriel grew up in the rural Mabouya Valley, where his family was engaged in a range of mostly agricultural pursuits. Excelling in school from a young age, he completed secondary school in the capital city, Castries, and obtained a post-secondary diploma in general agriculture in Guyana in the early 1990s. Before long, Gabriel, too—like his parents before him—was working the land, in tandem with some other ventures. He started a family and by the late 2000s had built what he thought was a stable livelihood for himself and his children. Then in 2010, hurricane Tomas struck St. Lucia, devastating the island and Gabriel's economic standing along with it.

It was in the context of this environmental and economic calamity that Gabriel applied to join the Seasonal Agricultural Worker Program, a migrant labour arrangement between Canada and a number of countries in the Caribbean basin, including St. Lucia, that brings upwards of forty thousand farm workers each year to work on Canadian farms and other agri-business operations for contracts lasting up to eight months. The SAWP was founded in 1966, the result of years of pressure from select Ontario farmers' associations and British colonies-turned-countries in the English-speaking Caribbean. Canada's eventual acquiescence to this lobbying was in large part the result of geopolitics. As countries in the Caribbean, Africa, and Asia gained their independence amid a global wave of decolonization in the decades following the Second World War, wealthy capitalist countries such as Canada were eager to cultivate diplomatic and economic relationships with their emerging counterparts, an objective that took on an even greater urgency in the context of the Cold War struggle for influence between capitalist and Communist blocs. In guest worker arrangements such as the SAWP, Canada and its fellow Commonwealth members in the Caribbean found an object of mutual interest. For Canada, the SAWP fulfilled diplomatic as well as domestic political aims, enabling the federal government to offer a concession to the important (and vocal) constituency of Ontario farmers. Sending countries were likewise happy to strengthen diplomatic ties, while also placing a high value on labour mobility schemes for their potential to alleviate un- and under-employment and inject foreign currency into local economies.

The SAWP started out as an agreement between Canada and Jamaica, bringing 264 Jamaicans to Canada in the pilot year of 1966. The next year, Barbados and Trinidad and Tobago joined the scheme, followed by Mexico in 1974, and eight Eastern Caribbean states, including St. Lucia, in 1976. The SAWP remained quite small in its first few decades, only exceeding six thousand workers once in its first twenty years of existence, and accounting for less than 10 percent of the agricultural wage labour force in Ontario, where nearly all the program's participants worked.[2] It surpassed this level in the late 1980s, aided by administrative changes to the scheme, and continued to expand over the subsequent years, albeit in fits and starts. It is really in the last two decades that the SAWP has ballooned in size. I argue elsewhere that this has occurred in conjunction with the hyper-consolidation of agriculture, resulting in the ever-greater domination of Canadian farming by heavily capitalized, scaled-up operations that can afford the higher up-front costs of employing guest workers compared to Canadians. (The terms of the SAWP require employers to provide accommodations and to foot part of the bill for workers' flights to Canada.)[3]

From day one, the SAWP was structured as an explicitly temporary labour migration scheme. While nothing in its initial arrangements announced it as such, the matter was quickly clarified when, in the program's first year, various stakeholders began inquiring about whether or not participants were welcome to stay in Canada to pursue full-time agricultural work, and were instructed by civil servants that any participant wishing to immigrate to Canada would need to return to Jamaica and apply "through the proper channels."[4] As Liberal member of Parliament (and parliamentary secretary to the minister of manpower and immigration) John Munro said in the House of

Commons in response to one such inquiry in October 1966: "These workers . . . cannot be accorded special treatment, because they came for seasonal work, on conditions strictly defined as temporary."[5] In his pathbreaking work on the history of the program's founding, sociologist Vic Satzewich demonstrated that a critical reason why the SAWP was structured as temporary was, simply, racism. Canadian officials were wary of permitting the permanent immigration of "unskilled" Black agriculturalists and hoped that by accepting a certain number of seasonal farm workers each year, they could dissuade Caribbean countries from pushing for more spots for permanent immigrants.[6] Indeed, during the second year of the SAWP in 1967, at the same time as one thousand West Indians were working on strictly temporary contracts in Ontario, the provincial Department of Agriculture and Food was launching a program to recruit *permanent* immigrant farm workers from the United Kingdom.[7]

SAWP participants' lack of access to permanent residency continues to this day. Of course, as civil servants' comments during the program's infancy indicated, nothing precludes SAWP workers from applying to immigrate to Canada via the various available channels. But as working people from rural areas, often without much formal education (or, in the case of Mexican workers, fluency in either of Canada's official languages), the overwhelming majority of program participants do not qualify for entry under the Federal Skilled Worker stream, or "points system." And the seasonality of their work—combined with the immense power wielded by employers—makes it difficult to qualify under other streams, such as the Provincial Nominee Program, in which year-round work and the nomination of an employer are requirements.[8] It comes as little surprise, then, that within the labyrinth of temporary foreign worker programs in Canada, workers in the SAWP have by far the lowest rate of conversion into permanent residents. After five years of experience in the SAWP, only 2 percent of workers have gained permanent residency, and after ten years, it's just 3.4 percent.[9] For nearly every participant in the SAWP, settling permanently in Canada remains far out of reach. Many labour for ten, twenty, or even thirty years in Canadian agriculture, but this experience gives them no credit towards achieving permanent residency. They are, in the words of one scholar, "permanently temporary."[10]

Gabriel was admitted into the SAWP in 2011 and travelled to Canada for his first contract early in 2012, thus beginning the odyssey that lies at the heart of this book. As Gabriel recounts in the pages to come, over the course of his first season in Canada, he came face to face with the many ways in which the structures of the SAWP serve to marginalize workers, not least of which is the near-total barring of permanent residency. These realizations, which flew in the face of Canada's pristine image in St. Lucia and much of the rest of the world, came to form part of what Gabriel labels the Twenty Injustices of Canada. Beyond the question of permanent status, workers in the SAWP are tied to a single employer, unable to freely choose or change who they work for. Those employers wield an immense amount of power over workers, and not only during the workday. Workers live in employer-provided housing, and they often find their social and private lives—where they go, who visits the bunkhouse, and so on—monitored and controlled by their bosses. Farmers also have the ability to request workers by name to return to their employ. Since not being "named" can cause a worker to miss a year of participation in the program, this adds to employers' power, providing a strong disincentive against voicing complaints, missing work for illness or injury, or otherwise drawing any sort of attention that suggests anything other than "model employee." A further disincentive against rocking the boat is the fact that employers enjoy essentially free rein to fire workers and send them back to their home countries should they be dissatisfied with them in any way. In the SAWP, then, farmers are not only participants' employers, but also their landlords and immigration agents. With such stark power imbalances, it is not surprising that instances of workplace abuse and abject working and living conditions are commonplace within the SAWP, as Gabriel quickly came to learn.

As far as we know, this book is the first published account of the life of a migrant farm worker in a Canadian temporary foreign worker program. But that is not to say that it stands alone. Instead, this project rests upon a decades-long tradition of activism and intellectual work by migrant workers and their allies that over time, in an arduous journey, has forced the conditions and struggles of these workers into the consciousness of Canadians and onto the political agenda. It is an effort that is still very much ongoing, and in which this book hopes to play a part. A particularly important inspiration to the present volume is Makeda Silvera's ground-breaking book *Silenced: Talks with Working Class West Indian Women about Their Lives and Struggles as Domestic Workers in Canada*, a collection of interviews with ten West Indian domestic workers in Canada, first published in 1983.[11] In providing a platform for domestic workers to present their lives and experiences in their own words, that book revealed the gross injustices and abuses of the scheme, but also the relentless persistence of domestic workers in pushing for better conditions and asserting their dignity and humanity in what was all too often a dehumanizing experience. We hope that this narrative will add Gabriel's voice to those of his domestic worker forerunners who so courageously put their voices on record some four decades ago, and that it will inspire other labour migrants—farm workers, caregivers, and others—to do the same.

This book's status as "first" unfortunately comes as little surprise. Not only does the structure of the SAWP make speaking out against the program's injustices extremely unappealing, it also tends, almost exclusively, to select participants with low levels of formal education, for whom writing or participating in the writing of a book would be a daunting undertaking. In this sense, Gabriel is perfectly positioned to be the person to break this barrier. Unusually for a participant in the SAWP, Gabriel completed not only secondary school but also a post-secondary diploma. Early in his adult working life, Gabriel taught in both primary and secondary schools. And though he did not continue in that profession, Gabriel has, really, never stopped teaching. During his first season in Canada, Gabriel's assisting of co-workers with paper-work and other matters made difficult by their low levels of literacy earned him the endearing nickname of "Teacher." In the years since, he has moved countless classrooms and audiences with his remarkable ability to convey the profound injustices faced by migrant workers in a way that is at once thoughtful, emotional, and engaging. With his ability to perfectly capture and express the experience and interests of migrant workers and their essential position within global capitalist food production, Gabriel might be considered—borrowing from the radical Italian political theorist Antonio Gramsci—an "organic intellectual" of Canada's migrant labour force.[12]

Gabriel's account is also special because of the way in which he understands and articulates his own life experiences within the broad historical sweep of Caribbean, Canadian, and world history. Through a deep engagement with the histories of slavery, indenture, imperialism, capitalism, and international relations, Gabriel puts forward an understanding of migrant worker programs that offers a strong rebuke to depictions of such programs as a form of "international aid." Against such interpretations, Gabriel's narrative shows how the SAWP forms part of a long history of racialized, unfree labour mobility schemes that have lain at the very heart of the development of global capitalism. Though the promoters of state-managed guest worker schemes such as the SAWP boast of the economic benefits to program participants, Gabriel and countless others have found instead that by far the greatest benefits accrue to agri-business, while workers find themselves dependent on continual participation in migrant labour in order to maintain a very modest livelihood, doing so at great cost to their bodies, minds, families, and relationships. As the US historian of migrant farm labour Cindy Hahamovitch insightfully frames it, Global South-North guest worker programs are indeed a form of foreign aid, but not in the direction typically understood. "Perversely," Hahamovitch writes, "sending countries sent foreign aid *to* the United States"—and, we might add, to Canada—"in the form of young men in their peak years of physical fitness." While "host" countries benefit from migrants' labour, they bear little to none of the costs of their upbringing, education, health care, or retirement.[13]

But Gabriel's story—and indeed the story of migrant workers writ large—is not one of totalizing exploitation and oppression. Though migrant workers in Canada face abhorrent conditions and daunting barriers to challenging them, they have never simply accepted their lot. Since the very first year of the SAWP, workers have stood up, asserted their dignity and humanity, and demanded better conditions from employers, the Canadian state, and home governments alike. In the program's first year, in 1966, five Jamaican workers of the Seventh-day Adventist faith refused to work on the Sabbath day, Saturday.[14] The next year, 1967, twenty Trinidadian tobacco workers staged wildcat strikes to protest poor conditions and unequal pay between Canadian and West Indian workers.[15] In the over five decades since, a panoply of protest has continued within the program, in defiance of the immense structural imbalances discouraging such acts. To be clear, these were by no means romantic stories of worker uprising; in most of these cases, the end result for participants in labour stoppage or other forms of protest was to be summarily deported to their home countries, and in at least some instances banished from future participation.[16] The other major historic group of migrant workers in Canada—domestic workers—also boast a long tradition of organization and resistance, in spite of their own daunting set of barriers to doing so.[17]

Like his forebears in domestic service and agriculture, Gabriel, too, refused to accept the conditions of "labour apartheid," as one scholar has called it.[18] Gabriel's activism began in his first year in Canada, when he attended a vigil for the ten Peruvian and Nicaraguan temporary foreign workers (and the Canadian truck driver) who were killed in a horrific highway accident in Hampstead, Ontario, in February 2012. Connecting this accident with his own early experiences in Canada, Gabriel began to develop an understanding of the structural oppression facing all migrant workers in Canada. Though he hadn't planned to do so, Gabriel felt moved to speak at this vigil, and delivered a powerful commentary on the migrant condition.[19] It was at this vigil that Gabriel first connected with Justicia (Justice) for Migrant Workers (J4MW), an organization that he would later join. This event, in a way, represented the start of Gabriel's journey as a migrant justice activist, though in order for him to fully utilize his voice, Gabriel would have to wait until he was no longer a SAWP participant, lest he risk the repatriation and banishment that was often the fate of "troublemakers" within the scheme. While resistance has been a constant feature of the SAWP throughout its history, first-hand accounts of those efforts are exceptionally rare, another part of what makes Gabriel's narrative so important.

◇◇◇

Gabriel and I first met in February 2016, when a group of migrant justice and labour activists, organized by Justicia for Migrant Workers, paid a visit to then immigration minister John McCallum's constituency office in Markham, Ontario, to deliver, on the occasion of Family Day, a photo collage of migrant workers and their families, in the shape of a broken heart, emblematic of the separation of migrant worker families. Part of the year-long Harvesting Freedom campaign marking the fiftieth anniversary of the SAWP, the Family Day delegation demanded that the Liberal government include temporary foreign workers in its pledge to facilitate family reunification within the immigration system. Gabriel gave a stirring speech to the small group of activists shivering in the cold outside McCallum's office that day, detailing the terrible conditions faced by migrant farm workers and rallying workers and allies to the long struggle that securing justice and dignity would entail. "We are asking for fairness," Gabriel declared in his closing remarks. "And where are we asking for fairness? . . . In a country that preaches fairness. And after fifty years, don't we deserve that?"

Gabriel and I continued to see each other at meetings and demonstrations in the months and years to come. In October 2017, I invited Gabriel to speak at an event on migrant labour in Canada that I was organizing as part of the Toronto Workers' History Project. At the time, he was working on a farm near Kitchener, so I drove him to and from the event in Toronto that evening. Those few hours in the car gave us a chance to speak at greater length and get to know each other a bit better. On the way back to Kitchener that night, after he had delivered yet another show-stopping talk, I asked Gabriel if he had ever considered writing a book. He said he hadn't given it much thought, but that he would keep it in mind. A year and a half later, I was teaching a course on the history of global migration at the University of Toronto Scarborough and invited Gabriel to give a guest lecture to the class. Again, he left his audience spellbound. We went for lunch afterwards and during our conversation I asked Gabriel if he remembered my previous suggestion about writing a book and whether he had given it any thought. He did remember, and indeed, in the meantime, someone else had had made the exact same suggestion to him. But he hadn't yet given it serious consideration. I reiterated my enthusiasm should he ever wish to pursue it and offered my support in any capacity.

A few days later, an email arrived in my inbox from Gabriel. "Regarding your suggestion about writing a book," he wrote, "I've given some thought to it. I am very inclined to take it on. Please guide me." I was thrilled. We met soon after and discussed some of the different ways such a project could be completed, ranging from Gabriel drafting a manuscript on his own to a collaborative process between the two of us, using oral history interviews. Gabriel chose the latter option, and over the next few months we charted a course of action. By September

2019, we were ready to get down to it and between then and February 2020, Gabriel and I sat down for eleven oral history interviews of about one hour each, which are the basis for the chapters that follow. After our superb research assistant, then–McGill student Megan Coulter, produced polished transcripts of these interviews, Gabriel and I decided on an overall structure for the book and worked together to draft it according to the following methodology: Using the transcripts, I drafted one chapter at a time and sent it to Gabriel for review. Gabriel would send feedback to me and then we would meet over Zoom and go through the chapter together, making adjustments and additions along the way. This was supplemented by frequent exchanges over WhatsApp and email. My contributions to the book also include the endnotes sprinkled throughout; these provide some additional historical context and point to further sources. From my point of view, our partnership has been one based on trust, mutual respect, and open communication, and I feel very lucky to have spent so much time with Gabriel, speaking with him and learning from him, throughout the process of writing this book.

◇◇◇

In the years since we first embarked on this project, Gabriel's story has only become more important. The COVID-19 pandemic that began in 2020 proved devastating to migrant farm workers in Canada, with thousands getting sick and at least four dying from the virus, a subject that Gabriel and I discuss in a conversation that forms the epilogue to this book.

Gabriel's story also contains important lessons for us as we confront an even greater global challenge than the coronavirus: the climate emergency. Gabriel's entrance into the SAWP came about primarily as a result of a hurricane that threw his life—and that of thousands of compatriots—into disarray. In our rapidly evolving climate, such storms are becoming more and more ferocious, and more and more people are being displaced by adverse weather events.[20] In other words, climate migrants like Gabriel are going to be an ever-more familiar sight the world over. Meanwhile, a key area of economic transformation needed to reduce greenhouse gases is in commercial agriculture, one of the biggest CO_2 emitters. The project of transforming agriculture into a more sustainable sector is one that, like such transformations in other sectors, will require massive amounts of labour.[21] But instead of having a stable, well-paid agricultural workforce that could spark this transition, Canada has a highly vulnerable, temporary farm workforce, the supply of which is easily disrupted by climate or health crises. This is a situation that should deeply trouble all Canadians.

◇◇◇

Gabriel's story puts a human face to the tens of thousands of migrant workers who toil annually in Canada's fields, factories, family homes, and fast-food restaurants. Valued for their labour but almost never welcome to join Canadian society ("good enough to work, but not good enough to stay," to invert a common refrain of activists), migrant workers often come off in public discourse as an undifferentiated mass, known purely as labourers rather than as human beings, an impression that the oft-used acronym TFW (temporary foreign worker) only further solidifies. Gabriel's story makes such an impression impossible. It is, among other things, a powerful assertion of dignity and humanity in the face of a migrant labour system that is all too often dehumanizing. It is a reminder, to any who should need it, that the men and women who grow our food, care for our elders and children, serve our meals, and perform so many other critical yet undervalued jobs are complex human beings, with families, friends, and communities, with ideas, with hopes and dreams, with innumerable skills, with so much to contribute to a society whose leaders—and some other members— have exhibited a stubborn callousness towards their well-being and their intrinsic value as human beings. Gabriel's account also shows how migrant workers, from their very first arrivals in Canada, have refused to accept the marginalized position that they've been placed in. This book tells the story of Gabriel's lifelong struggle—part of the centuries-long struggle of unfree labour migrants the world over—to harvest freedom.

Part One

A Child of History

Chapter 1
WELCOME TO CANADA

I left my home in St. Lucia for Canada under the cover of darkness and arrived on the farm in Canada, which was to be my home and workplace for the next eight months, under the cover of darkness twenty-four hours later.

Early in the morning of the previous day, January 17, 2012, I jumped out of my bed, full of nervous energy, to embark on a long but significant journey in my life, a journey that would test and ultimately transform various aspects of my physical, spiritual, financial, and social life. The first flight was to sunny Barbados, where my companions and I, sixteen of us migrant farm workers from St. Lucia, spent a long day in the airport, anxiously waiting for our evening flight to Toronto, making the best of it by watching cricket on television at the airport bar and slowly getting to know one another.

It was only during the long layover in the Barbados airport that my early-morning excitement began to give way to some more conflicted feelings about the journey I was on. In other words, reality began to set in. That day was a mental war zone for me, with half of my brain telling me to go to Canada and the other half telling me to stay. Holding me back were the uncertainties of travelling to a new country to work in a program that I knew little about, and leaving behind everything I had and everyone I knew—most importantly, my two children, Gania, thirteen, and Christi, eleven, during the critical adolescent stage.

On the other hand, I was pushed forward by my burning desire to experience commercial agriculture, my dire financial situation, and the hope that working in Canada might provide a solution to my predicament.

Finally, it was time to leave Barbados and board the flight to Toronto. The battle to calm my mind continued during that five-hour flight. Conversations with the two newfound friends and colleagues I was seated between couldn't calm my thoughts and fears in anticipation of the unknown. Nor could the in-flight entertainment.

At last, we landed at Pearson airport in Toronto, went through immigration, and were met by a member of the diplomatic corps of the Organization of Eastern Caribbean States—of which St. Lucia is a member—who was to serve as our liaison officer during our stay in Canada. Dressed in a stylish, long, and expensive-looking winter coat, the liaison officer addressed us in the diplomatic language common to such officials, offering us words that he intended to be comforting, welcoming, and reassuring.

But if any of us were reassured, it wore off quickly. The moment we stepped out of the airport and into the cold, mid-January night, we realized that we did not have the appropriate clothing to face the winter. In the long process of applying to and joining the program, no government official had prepared us for this crucial fact, let alone supplied us with any winter clothing. In that moment, the bitterly cold wind felt like a hard slap in the face.

Relief from the cold would not come any time soon. The bus that had been sent to take us to our assigned farm in Leamington, Ontario, did not have functioning heating. For a full four hours, as the clock ticked past midnight and into the early morning hours, we sat on the freezing, dark bus as it lumbered west down the 401, shivering and wondering what we had gotten ourselves into.

Things did not improve upon arrival at the farm. When we finally got there at around three o'clock in the morning, the driver dropped us off at the wrong bunkhouse. It was empty, the beds were all turned upside down, and worst of all—after four hours in a freezing bus—the heat was not on.

The farm office was closed and no one was inside. The bus driver had already left. We were in a new place in a new country, in the middle of the night in the dead of winter. We had no choice but to wait in the frigid bunkhouse until seven in the morning, when the sun peeked above the horizon and workers on the farm began to stir. Only then were we finally directed to our correct bunkhouse, which, to our great relief, had functioning heating.

For me and my fifteen companions, this was our welcome to Canada. If our welcome was that rough, I wondered, was I really ready to face what was in store for me?

◇◇◇

My welcome to Canada contrasted sharply with the ideas of the country I had held up to that point—especially growing up. Throughout my schooling in St. Lucia, Canada was presented as a place of high standards. We admired Canada for its economy, education, health care, diversity, human rights record, and agriculture. We were impressed by its expansive and beautiful geography.

Coming from a small, developing island country, seemingly nowhere on the map and known principally for its bananas and beaches, Canada stood out not only as an example to look up to, but as almost a paradise: a site of refuge, a champion of human rights, the ideal place to raise a family. Growing up, I never heard anything bad or sad about Canada. And as the saying goes, no news is good news.

Canada also played an active role in development projects in St. Lucia, something that directly benefited me as an adolescent. The last secondary school that I attended, the Castries Comprehensive Secondary School (CCSS), was, in fact, a gift from Canada, built by the Canadian International Development Agency (CIDA) and opened in 1976. It was a "comprehensive" secondary school, a higher academic level than a normal high school, and very well equipped.

By gifting my secondary school, Canada helped me at that stage in my life to have a decent standard of living, opening the door to employment and educational opportunities in St. Lucia that otherwise would not have been available to me.

The Seasonal Agricultural Worker Program (SAWP)—the migrant farm worker program in which I would later take part—also had a very positive reputation in St. Lucia. It was yet another example of Canada's generosity and the economic opportunities available there.

I first heard about the program as a child. At that time, in the late 1970s, in my family home in rural Mabouya Valley, we did not have electricity. Because this was typical of most families in the country-side, it was common practice for neighbours to come together in the evening at the home of someone who had electricity, and especially television or radio. People would either socialize or listen to programs that they were interested in. In this way, my mother would often take me and my siblings to a neighbour's house, where we would play with the other children while the adults chatted, listened to the radio, and so on.

During these evenings at neighbours' homes, I remember hearing over the radio about people signing up for the "farm program," which meant both the Canadian program as well as a similar arrangement with the United States. The Labour Department would use the radio to call out the names of workers who had been selected, instructing them to come down to the ministry to complete their paperwork and the like. When these bulletins came on the radio, the grown-ups would often comment on how the program had benefited the families of participating workers. The way my elders spoke about it, being in the program sounded like an immense privilege.

Just like with Canada as a whole, I never heard anything bad about the program. And again, I figured that no news is good news. Over the course of that long, freezing first night in Canada, my perception of the country began to crack. In the coming months and years, it would shatter.

But before we get to all that, we need to start at the beginning, in St. Lucia.

Chapter 2
BEGINNINGS

I was born in 1971 in Mabouya Valley, St. Lucia. St. Lucia is a small, mountainous, and stunningly beautiful island in the Eastern Caribbean, just forty-three kilometres long and twenty-three kilometres wide, and with a population of only 180,000.

Colonized multiple times by both the French and English, St. Lucia finally ended up as a British colony in 1814, only gaining its full independence a century and a half later, in 1979, when I was seven years old. We still have strong French influences in our culture and British influences in our institutions. Our systems of government, law, and education, for example, are very much carry-overs from our British colonial past.[22]

While agriculture (first sugar and then bananas) has been the main driver of St. Lucia's economy for most of the past four hundred years, in recent decades tourism has taken its place. If you've ever seen a photograph of St. Lucia, it was most likely a classic tourism-promotion image of a pristine beach with light blue-green water and spectacular, steep green mountains rising up in the background.

I come from a part of St. Lucia that does not show up in the tourism brochures, even though it is not far from the coast. The Mabouya Valley—also called Dennery Valley—is a major agricultural area on the eastern side of the island, separated from the capital Castries, on the west coast, by a majestic, uninhabited mountain range that runs down the centre of the island. To reach the capital from the valley requires you to travel a steep, narrow, and winding road that climbs and then descends the mountains. The small village where I grew up is called Derniere Riviere.

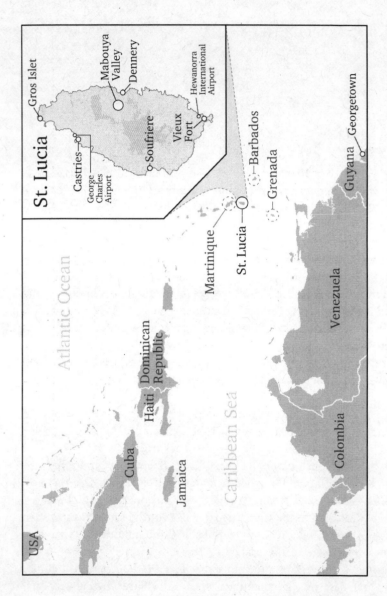

The Caribbean and St. Lucia. Map by Nate Wessel.

8   **Harvesting Freedom**

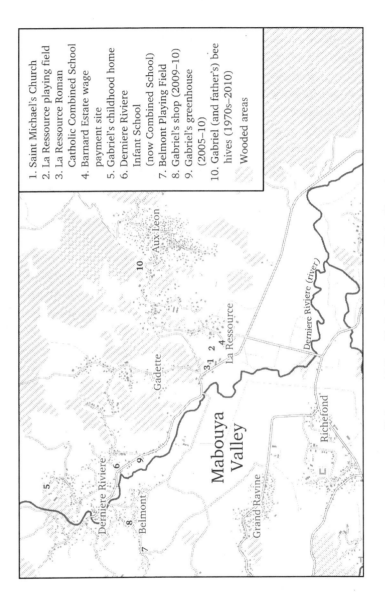

1. Saint Michael's Church
2. La Ressource playing field
3. La Ressource Roman Catholic Combined School
4. Barnard Estate wage payment site
5. Gabriel's childhood home
6. Derniere Riviere Infant School (now Combined School)
7. Belmont Playing Field
8. Gabriel's shop (2009–10)
9. Gabriel's greenhouse (2005–10)
10. Gabriel (and father's) bee hives (1970s–2010)
    Wooded areas

Mabouya Valley, St. Lucia. Map by Nate Wessel.

I was the second youngest of my mother and father's nine children, although my father had more—seventeen in total. My mother was my father's second wife; his other children came from previous relationships.

My mother's name was Dora. My father, who was twenty-two years her senior and sixty years old when I was born, was named Fitz. Both of their life stories are deeply interwoven with the history of St. Lucia.

◇◇◇

My father was of Asian descent, and my mother was of African descent. That goes back to our history. All the islands in the Caribbean, including St. Lucia, were colonized. In St. Lucia, the main economic activity undertaken by colonists was sugar production. And plantation owners brought in Africans to do this work as slaves. My mother is a direct descendant of these people. After emancipation, which happened in 1838 in the British West Indies and 1848 in the French West Indies, the freed slaves had an option whether to continue to work on the plantation or to go on their own, to make their own living off the land. Because of the barbaric nature of slavery and rough treatment on the estates, most of them chose to go on their own. As a result, the plantation owners were left with a problem: they didn't have enough workers. So they went to Asia, to bring in indentured workers. And my father is a descendant of these people.

This is a history that is better known in places like Trinidad and Guyana, whose populations are roughly 50 percent Indian and 50 percent people of African descent. But in St. Lucia, only a small percentage of our population is of Indian descent—2 percent identify as East Indian and another 11 percent as "mixed," many of whom have Indian ancestry. The community of Belmont (where I would live as an adult, across the river from Derniere Riviere) was one of the few places in St. Lucia where Indians settled, coming originally to work on the nearby plantation. The amazing thing about people of Indian descent in St. Lucia is that they've been integrated. There are lots of people like me, who are of both of Indian and African descent. But it took a lot of time for that integration to take place.

So I carry one leg of the indentured worker and another leg of the slave. In coming to Canada, I found myself participating in yet another exploitative labour migration movement, one that, like these older movements, features people of colour. In this way, like my mother and father, I, too, am wrapped up in a much larger history.

◇◇◇

St. Lucia was seven times colonized by France and seven times by England, a history that you can see in the country's place names and language. St. Lucia's capital city and the three other main towns all have French names: Castries (the capital), Gros Islet, Vieux Fort, and Soufriere. Other places have English names, such as Rodney Bay, Pigeon Island, or Belmont.

In terms of language, especially in the countryside, we use a spoken language based on French but with borrowed elements from African and Indigenous Caribbean languages, Spanish, and English. This language goes by many names: some call it Creole (sometimes spelled Kwéyòl), others call it broken French, still others call it patois (or sometimes patwa). To the average person in the countryside, Creole is the mother tongue because it is the spoken language in the house. English is like a second language. England was the last to colonize us, so the English influences on Creole came last. So on paper we are English, but in practice, in the countryside especially, we are still French. In school you speak English, but when you go home you speak Creole.

It is often said in St. Lucia that three Cs were used to colonize us: cane, Christianity, and cricket. In some ways, this saying is a watered down version of our past that leaves out the violence and genocide of colonialism (whose perpetrators devastated first the Indigenous peoples who had called St. Lucia home for some 3,500 years before the arrival of Europeans, and then the thousands of enslaved Africans and their descendants who produced the wealth of the sugar colony for over a century before emancipation). Yet the three Cs do point out some pillars of St. Lucian culture, history, and economic life.

Those three Cs came together very strongly in our community and in my father's life. Sugar cane production was now mostly historical, but Christianity and cricket were very much alive.

There was only one Catholic Church in the Mabouya Valley, St. Michael's, which was located in La Ressource, just a couple of kilometres from Derniere Riviere. When I was growing up, most of our population identified as Catholic, and St. Michael's was the heart of the community. (In recent years, Protestant churches—especially Seventh-day Adventist and Pentecostal—have flourished, drawing many St. Lucians away from the Catholic faith.)

Before St. Michael's was built, the closest church was in Dennery Village, and people would have to walk for hours to get there for church services, first communions, baptisms, and so on. I heard stories growing up about people who did not have shoes or slippers and had to tie a mango seed under each foot to walk, because the road was so hot during the heat of the day.

St. Michael's is a huge building, made of stones. Those stones were set by volunteer labour from the community. So the church's design is very different from other churches. It represents community participation. This project really united people, as they contributed to building something central to the community.

On Sundays, after mass, people would congregate in that area and socialize. The school, now called La Ressource Roman Catholic Combined School, was right next to the church, as was the playing field. Cricket matches, which were often held on Sundays after mass, were another important place for socializing. Cricket really brought the community together. The church was also close to the location that the local estate (which switched from sugar cane to bananas in the 1950s and 60s) used to distribute workers' pay every Friday. So this part of the valley was an important area for socializing.

My father was born in 1911. In his youth he was a talented cricketer, making him quite popular as a young man. When I was growing up, even though my father was by then in his sixties and seventies, his exploits on the cricket field were still widely remembered.

In his working life, my father was a supervisor on the estate that extended throughout the Mabouya Valley, further raising his esteem in the community. The estate dated back to the colonial era, when it was worked by enslaved people and later by indentured labourers. In my father's time, it was owned by Denis Barnard, whose forebears had acquired it sometime in the mid-nineteenth century, after emancipation. After his death, the estate passed to Barnard's children.

My father would later develop his own business interests, becoming a banana farmer, beekeeper, and carpenter. This was the work he did by the time I was born. Growing up, people told me that our house was the first in the area to have a roof made of galvanized zinc. Prior to that point, all the houses had thatched roofs.

All these things—his cricketing career, his work on the estate, his entrepreneurship, and also his large family—made my father a leader within our community. People in the community often turned to him for emergency financial assistance. He also frequently employed community members.

One way of measuring his stature is that he was godfather to eighty-one children over the course of his life. This was also a reflection of his role within the church, since the tradition of godparents was in part a religious one.

My mother, on the other hand, took care of the house and children, which was a common thing in the countryside. I remember her being very meticulous with all the work she did around the house. By the time I was old enough to remember, my mother and father had separated, so I grew up without a father figure in the house. I mostly saw my father on the weekends when I would help him with various chores related to his many business interests.

And though my father did provide us with some support, my mother still had her fair share of hardship as a single mother and head of the household. We did not have electricity, a gas stove, or running water, but there were always bills to pay, with living and educational expenses being priorities.

My mother being a housewife meant that my food was prepared, my clothes were washed and folded, and so on. But, because I was a boy, she never taught me how to do those things, as was common practice in the countryside. (I did learn some cooking skills on the weekends at my father's place, though, where I was often tasked with preparing meals.)

My mother paid close attention to our education. She insisted that we speak English at home, which went against the norm in the countryside, and ensured that we were regular and punctual for school.

My mother was a very social and community-minded person. She had lots and lots of friends. The community was very friendly and social, and it was common for people to come and spend time at our home, which my mother took great pleasure in. Laughter, joking, and the latest gossip always filled the home. People also sought out my mother to get her help with reading and writing letters. And she was always happy to share traditional medicines with friends and neighbours.

My mother was a devout Catholic. We went to mass nearly every Sunday, and my mother was insistent on us children receiving the sacraments of baptism and first communion.

An important part of my mother's philosophy involved food. My mother believed in cooking more food than we needed so that in the event that a stranger stopped by, we would have something to offer them. Sometimes in my family we saw this as wasteful, but to her, food was neither privilege nor commodity for profit. Rather, it was a basic right and not something you should keep away from anybody.

My mother was such a good cook that she was often asked to cook for special celebrations such as baptisms or weddings. She is still remembered for her style of dumplings, a popular St. Lucian dish prepared on special occasions.

My mother was also passionate about politics and cultural activities. In St. Lucia there are two traditional flower festivals: La Rose, which is celebrated in August, and La Marguerite, in October. The festivals, which go back as far as the eighteenth century, derive from a mix of African and European traditions. They are Catholic celebrations, with La Rose named for St. Rose of Lima, and La Marguerite named for St. Marguerite.

The two festivals and the people who participate in them are considered (friendly) rivals, but my mother identified with both of them and participated in both festivals. (There is no easy way to describe how some people come to be a Rose and others a Marguerite. People born between January and August tend to be Roses, while those born later in the year tend to be Marguerites. But there is no rigid rule about this, and people simply pick one over the other, or, in the case of my mother, pick both.)[23]

The celebrations were a reflection of society, and each year there were participants who portrayed a king, queen, prince, princess, doctor, and magistrate, as well as nurses, policemen, and soldiers. My mother devoted a lot of her time to creating the elaborate decorations featured in the festivities.

Preparations for the festivals began months in advance. People would meet on Friday evenings, a gathering called "sayas," to plan, practise, create decorations, raise funds, and recruit participants. My mother was passionately involved in all of this.

Both of these festivals revolved around music. St. Lucia has many musical traditions, including solo, kont, kwadril, and bélé. As part of these festivals, brave and passionate people like my mother would often write and sing songs about current events and gossip, songs that would poke fun at members of the rival group. These singers are called "chantwelles."

She also loved country music, which was imported from the United States but has become a major part of St. Lucia's musical culture. In fact, when George Jones, the father of country music, passed away, it was said to be a bigger deal in St. Lucia than in his home country of the United States.

◇◇◇

The many lessons I learned from my parents—social skills, commitment to education, English-language ability, punctuality, and so much more—have helped me at every stage of my life. Not only in my school days, but also later on, as a migrant farm worker and in my transition to permanent residency in Canada. And even more so nowadays, in my work as an organizer with Justicia (Justice) for Migrant Workers (J4MW), outreach worker, and advocate for migrant workers in Canada, calling for Status for All.

Chapter 3
GROWING UP

I grew up in a big family. We were seven boys and two girls living with my mother. We lived way up a steep hill, at the time known as Morne Caca Cochon, but now called Austin Hill.

For as long I can remember, I was called by the nickname "Ricky." This is common practice in St. Lucia; literally everybody has a nickname that is completely different from their Christian name.

Our living conditions were fairly typical of people living in the countryside in those days. We had no running water or flush toilet. Pit toilets were the norm in the countryside. We had no electricity either. We lit the house by kerosene lamp and sometimes candles. Our house had four bedrooms, so we had to share among us. Privacy was not a luxury we could enjoy.

Our wooden home was at the entrance of my family's three-acre farm, situated on moderately sloping land that bounded with a river at the bottom of the slope, maybe five hundred metres from the house. The main crop we cultivated was bananas, but around our home were also lots of tropical fruit trees, such as cashew nuts, coconuts, a variety of citrus, golden apples, gooseberries, and a few varieties of mangoes. This was typical in the countryside, to have fruit trees around the house. As children, we had basically unlimited, year-round access to free fruits from these trees, a luxury I missed greatly when I moved to Castries for school as a teenager.

The three acres that we cultivated were on lands owned by the family of my father's first wife. We did not have formal ownership but had informal permission from that family to occupy and work the land. Arrangements like these are common in St. Lucia and throughout the English-speaking Caribbean.

We also raised animals, as was common practice in the country-side. We kept chickens, generally as a source of protein in our diet, and pigs, which were usually reserved for religious holiday celebrations like Easter, Christmas, or New Year's Day. And when we raised cows, it was generally our emergency fund: cows could be raised quickly and cheaply, and if we found ourselves strapped for cash they were easily sold for a good return on investment. Occasionally, we raised goats and sheep. They were slower-growing than cows and pigs so they weren't as attractive an investment, but they were helpful in controlling grass and weeds around the farm: we like to call them St. Lucian lawnmowers.

Because my mom was a single parent, my older siblings would take on work to help support the family. My siblings' work helped me to stay in school as the second youngest in the family. This was very fortunate for me. If I had been one of the oldest children instead of one of the youngest, the burden of work might have fallen on my shoulders instead.

After my parents separated, my contact with my father was mostly limited to weekends, but my eldest brother on my mom's side, Victor, became a father figure to me. It's not just that he helped provide for the family. It was also his personality.

Victor was an extrovert. He was always on the go, and there was never a dull moment with him. He was very active in the community. I felt like he was never home and that he only came home to sleep late at night. The very few times we were lucky to meet him at home, it felt like he wouldn't be there for long, like he had just come home to shower, get dressed, and get back on the go. He loved being with friends. He was active and popular as a scout leader in the community. Later he became a teacher, firefighter, bartender at a hotel, and a Rastafarian. In his own way, he touched so many lives so deeply.

Growing up in the countryside, there were certain tasks that we children had to do. Some of the daily chores included fetching water, washing dishes, sweeping the yard, and feeding the chickens and pigs. Other chores—such as fetching wood from the forest—took longer and were usually done on Saturday, the one day of the week that we were neither in school nor at church.

Fetching water was an especially important daily chore. Since our home did not have running water, we had to get water from the standpipes. These were public pipes fitted with taps that provided drinking water to our community, where homes were not connected to a public water system. The installation of standpipes was a major government campaign in the years surrounding independence that aimed to provide an alternative to dangerous and sometimes deadly river water (as you'll see below). The fact that we lived on a hill made fetching water even more difficult at times. During the dry season, when the water level was lowest, we would have to go farther to get water because the water didn't have enough pressure from gravity to come up the hill. So going to the standpipe to get fresh water was part of my upbringing.

We also helped out in the family garden (a fruit and vegetable plot), which was located miles away in the forest reserve (on Crown land). In our garden, we cultivated lots of yams and other root crops, some plantains, and tree crops like cocoa and breadfruit. Despite the garden being far and uphill, the shade from the canopy of the forest trees and the constant crossing of the river and its many tributaries made the journey bearable. We added to our fun by fishing for crabs, crayfish, and occasionally eels along our journey—without any fishing gear. The produce we grew was mainly for the Saturday market, in Castries.

We children also had to go to the forest to collect dry wood for cooking fuel. This was our least favourite chore. The majority of the people in my community did not have a stove, so the forest was their source of fuel. Because so many families relied on the forest for firewood, we would have to go farther and farther each time to get wood. We would often have to climb up tall trees to break off dry branches, which could be quite difficult.

Gardening and collecting wood were two ways that we—and many other families in our community—made use of public lands. But the practices also put a huge amount of pressure on the natural environment. Like us, many other families also planted gardens in the forest reserve. The common method of clearing the land for cultivation is slash and burn. Combined with cutting down trees for firewood, this not only reduced the forest vegetation, but also compromised the reserve's natural water catchment, via erosion.

Despite the best efforts of forest rangers to discourage people from these practices, people continued to clear-cut. There were three main reasons for this. First was poverty, meaning that many people had no other choice but to use the forest for survival. Second was ignorance; most people had no idea that their exploitation of the forest would have severe long-term consequences. The third and final reason for clear-cutting was the legacy of slavery and colonialism. After emancipation, freed slaves were not provided with any land from which to earn their livelihood and there was no significant change in the ownership of prime land: the colonizers kept their lands. It was in this context that practices of ad hoc deforestation began, practices that continued until very recently. Fortunately, in recent years, the government has developed much more effective conservation policies, including finding other lands where people from Derniere Riviere can farm.

Some of our chores, such as clothes washing, would bring us to the river. And sometimes we would play in the river on our way to or from collecting wood.

Water is life. The river was extremely important to us for washing, bathing, fishing, and water for irrigation, among other things. But all of that came at a great cost to my family.

The river was highly infested with parasitic worms that caused a disease called schistosomiasis, or bilharzia. A lot of people in the countryside got sick and were hospitalized because of this. One time, when I was a toddler, my entire family was hospitalized with bilharzia, and my brother Herald ("Errol") died as a result of the disease. He was seven years old.

That was a wake-up call to my family and the community about the dangers of bilharzia. Though this was a widespread problem and we knew of many people who had gotten sick, we never imagined that someone in our family or community would die as a result. Bilharzia was such a serious threat that the government launched a major program to combat it. And as a result of the bilharzia crisis, the government was compelled to provide pipe-borne water to the affected communities to dissuade people from going to the river for daily water use.

There were other dangers in our day-to-day lives. One that I came in contact with was pesticides. We used a variety of pesticides—especially herbicides—on our family farm. Like most farming families, we stored these chemicals in the home, and they often were not in a secure place, since there was little awareness of the dangers posed by these chemicals. One day when I was a child, I came across a Coca-Cola bottle that looked like it had Coke in it. It turns out that it was not Coke at all, but Gramoxone, a very common herbicide. As children often do, I shook up the bottle, hoping to make the Coke spray. I ended up getting Gramoxone in my eyes.

I immediately flushed my eyes with water, but it was not enough, and this incident caused me a lot of problems with my eyes, problems that last to this day. My eyes were red and runny for months after the accident. And even now, my eyes are not as clear as they used to be or as the average person's. This would not be my last exposure to pesticides: as I would learn many years later, unsafe pesticide use is not only a problem in developing countries but also in the world's richest ones.

◇◇◇

While we children busied ourselves with chores on Saturdays, for my mother, Saturday was market day. She would travel to Castries by a privately operated truck that carried passengers and cargo, a common mode of transportation in the St. Lucian countryside at that time, to sell ground provisions (root crops), green bananas, plantains, and other fruits that we grew on our farm. On market day, my mother would also buy supplies for the week with the proceeds from her sales.

When she returned on Saturday evening, she would always bring us something from the city. We would get a cake or even a packet of biscuits which we shared. It was always something different, and we really looked forward to that very special treat.

◇◇◇

Despite our family's economic difficulties, we still enjoyed a happy childhood. My siblings and I, along with other children from the area, entertained ourselves with all sorts of games and activities. Marbles was a big one. We also played hide and seek, and played with simple toys that we fashioned of wood. Our house had the only swing in the vicinity, making it a popular place for neighbourhood children to visit. We also enjoyed collecting cashews from a huge tree we had in our yard and drying them in the sun, a strong tradition in the countryside.

None of these activities had anything to do with electronics. With most of the games that we played, you had to socialize with other people and not just be on your own with an electronic device, as is common with children—and even adults—nowadays. The many games and the many things that we did together allowed us to develop strong and powerful bonds. To this day my siblings and I keep in touch with our childhood friends from the neighbourhood, even though we have gone our separate ways.

Chapter 4
EDUCATION

At the age of five, I started school in my home village of Derniere Riviere. The school was called an "infant school," and children usually attended until the age of ten or so, when they would move on to the primary school at La Ressource.

I had some advantages at home that really helped me to do well in school. A significant one is that there was some English influence in my family and we spoke some English at home, which is not a very common thing in the countryside. Most children arrived at school from families that only spoke Creole at home, and it was very hard for them to adjust to the teacher speaking only in English. You could see those children—who were the majority—struggling with their classwork, homework, punctuality, consistency, all of those things.

The children who struggled came mostly from poor families. Poverty was rampant in our community, a direct legacy of colonialism and slavery, but also the product of our political system, which is more interested in protecting the status quo than in improving the lives of ordinary St. Lucians. Many children would come to school without having eaten, and there were no meals provided at school. The poor children were often marked by their possessions. Whereas better-off kids would bring lunch in proper food containers made of stainless steel or aluminum, poorer kids, if they had lunch at all, might have it in a reused tin milk can. And poorer children often could not afford shoes and came to school instead in flip-flops—what we call slippers. On rainy days, you'd see a lot of dirt on the backs of their uniforms, kicked up by the slippers.

Another important advantage I had is that while children were often taken out of school to help on their family farms, I can count on my hands the number of times that this happened to me. This was partly because of my place in my family's birth order. It was also because of my mother's commitment to the education of her children. So these things together really helped me to get a decent foundation in education.

I transferred to La Ressource Primary School earlier than most students, around age nine. La Ressource had a reputation for having better teachers, who mostly came from outside of the community. For this reason, my mother was eager for me to benefit from this higher level of education.

The school was co-educational, but the teacher divided us into groups of boys and girls to encourage competition and stimulate learning. La Ressource was the first place I really remembered building some confidence. While my classmates always outperformed me in English and spelling, I was able to outperform them in mathematics.

In St. Lucia, at age twelve, students write the Common Entrance Exam in order to enter secondary school. When I was that age, in the 1980s, the island had very limited secondary school places, so you had to be among the best to get a chance to attend. Those who were not able to get a spot in secondary school continued in primary school until age fifteen, when they graduated. Similar education systems can be found throughout the English-speaking Caribbean, another legacy of British colonialism.

I cannot remember my exact score on the Common Entrance Exam, but I believe it was average and I barely made it to secondary school. The secondary school that I first attended, in Dennery Village, was called Dennery Junior Secondary School (DJSS). "Junior secondary" meant that it was not a full-fledged secondary school; it only lasted three years instead of the five years of a secondary school.

I struggled at first at DJSS but managed overall. Then something happened that filled me with confidence. In fact, I literally bought my confidence. Let me explain. One teacher, Ms. Paula Dash, who taught Cooperative Education, organized a "cooperative bank" within the school. Students were encouraged to deposit money in the bank and build their savings. As an incentive, a prize was presented at the end of the school year, at graduation, for the student who had saved the most money. Students also participated in running the bank: bookkeeping, processing deposits and withdrawals, and so on. Because I volunteered at the bank, I was able to see who had saved the most money. Evidently, I didn't know about confidentiality back then! But because I was able to see the competition, I could see exactly how much I needed to save to win the prize. So I worked my way up, and sure enough, at graduation, I won the prize. That was the first time I ever got a prize from school and it gave me a lot of confidence, even if I had purchased it!

Before that, the closest that I ever got to getting a reward at school was on a morning of our weekly assembly at the DJSS when the principal offered a ten-dollar reward after he noticed that no one from the three hundred or so students knew who the chair of the national independence day organizing committee for that year was. To me, back then, raising my hand was an opportunity to speak in public. Something I dreaded. I nervously and somewhat reluctantly answered, remembering that the chairperson was named Mr. Glasgow (I couldn't remember his first name, Austin).

The principal, Mr. Luke V. Girrard, was either amazed or taken aback that I was the only one to know something that was so national and ought to be common knowledge. With St. Lucia's independence still being so recent—just a handful of years prior, in 1979—the annual independence day celebrations were a big deal, even more so to students, who received a government-funded treat on that day. So the chair of the committee, Mr. Glasgow, was someone who was often in the news and was widely known. Despite the principal's promise of a ten-dollar reward, to my complete surprise, he said he did not have any cash with him that day. Worse yet, he did not promise to award me the prize money later. Instead of leaving my first opportunity to speak in public on a high note, I felt deflated.

At junior secondary school, I also remember having a brush with corporal punishment, which was common in schools in St. Lucia and throughout the Caribbean. The philosophy was "spare the rod, spoil the child," and indeed we children tended to see our teachers more as disciplinarians than educators. My own experience with corporal punishment happened when I was thirteen or fourteen and an altar boy. One Sunday, a fellow altar boy wrote a bunch of uppercase letters, in vertical order along the left margin of a sheet of paper, and showed it to me: H-M-M-D-Y-M-T-T-M-Y. He drew a line below it and asked me to write a number on it.

I assumed this was a serious activity, not only because he was an altar boy like me, but because he was my senior, very friendly, and—best of all—he lived with the priest. I can't remember what number I put, but let's say ten.

"Your mother took ten men to make you," he said.

"What?" I asked, confused.

"How Many Men Did Your Mother Take to Make You?" asked the boy, explaining what the letters stood for.

I thought that was pretty funny, so the next day at school I pulled the same trick on a friend of mine. But she didn't see any humour in it. She took it seriously and reported me. The principal didn't see any humour in it either (nor did he remember that he still owed me ten dollars!), and I was strapped on my back with a leather belt. That was my first—and only—experience of corporal punishment in school.

In the final year of junior secondary school, students got another chance to enter a full-fledged secondary school by writing an exam called the Common Middle Exam. I cannot remember my score, but I think it was average again. I was very much on the borderline and was fortunate to make it into Castries Comprehensive Secondary School, located in the capital city, Castries. The "comprehensive" in the school's name referred to the wide variety of courses that the school offered, in both technical and academic subjects.

Attending CCSS was the first time that Canada entered my life in a big way, since the school was a gift from Canada to St. Lucia, part of CIDA's Caribbean aid program.[24] The school opened in 1976, interestingly, the same year that the SAWP expanded to include St. Lucia and other Eastern Caribbean countries.

"Compre," as we called the school for short, was proud of its Canadian connection. The school's logo and uniforms had a red and white colour scheme, reflecting the colours of the Canadian flag.

Compre was well equipped, with experienced and qualified teachers, and offered subjects that other schools didn't offer. It consistently ranked among the best schools in terms of scores on the Caribbean Examinations Council (CXC, a standardized final exam administered throughout the English-speaking Caribbean).

By providing this top-of-the-line school to St. Lucia, Canada gave me the opportunity, in a very real way, to improve my standard of living. Little did I know, at that stage in my life, how big a role Canada would come to play in my life and how much more complicated my relationship with the country would get.

◇◇◇

It was too costly for me to commute to school in Castries every day from Derniere Riviere. Fortunately, my mother's sister, Mary Glasgow (or Aunty Helen as I called her) lived in Castries, and her family gave me a place to stay during the school week throughout my studies. I spent weekends at home in Derniere Riviere.

I started at CCSS at age fifteen, in 1986. Moving from the countryside to the city was a big adjustment. It blew my mind. It is like moving from a developing country to a developed country.

Three things I remember noticing very early were first, how in the countryside it was so easy to get fruits and vegetables for free, but in the city, you had to pay for everything. Second, English was the main spoken language in the city, in contrast to the predominantly Creole-speaking countryside. Sometimes people in Castries would call people like me from the countryside "country bookies," a derogatory term that suggested that Creole-speaking rural people were too crude to be in the city. Third, it was breathtaking to see huge cruise ships docking in the Castries harbour and to see crowds of white tourists downtown, where they were a big boost to the local economy. In the Mabouya Valley it had been very unusual to see a white person, and our communities were not involved in the tourism industry.

The adjustment was also difficult at school, where I was suddenly in the same classroom with students from better-off families, who had better English and a better academic foundation in general. Coming from a junior secondary school, some subjects were entirely new to me. And teachers' expectations were much higher.

My situation did not make it easy for me to meet these expectations because my weekends were not spent studying. Back home in Derniere Riviere, Saturdays were devoted to chores, including gardening and beekeeping. On Sundays we spent the better part of the morning at church and the better part of the afternoon travelling back to Castries. Public transportation—the same privately owned trucks and vans that my mother used to get to market—was very unreliable on Sundays. This is in stark contrast to Friday afternoons, when it was extremely busy in Castries because it was payday for the thousands of farmers who were cashing in on the banana boom of the mid-1980s, when we enjoyed preferential access to European markets and the crop was called "green gold." On Fridays, it was always a rush to get a seat on the public bus up to the countryside after a week of school in the city.

But I made some good friends who made adjusting much easier. And Aunty Helen was also very helpful and guided me a lot.

After my first year at CCSS I had to pick subject areas to focus on for my final two years at school. These would be the subjects I'd be tested on for the final CXC exams.

The most important subject to me was agriculture. Agriculture was my passion, a passion that had been awakened in me through working alongside my father—especially with beekeeping. Through beekeeping, I became aware of the role of weather in agriculture and the close relationship between the two. In St. Lucia, we have two rainy seasons. The first one is in the spring, after the dry, drought-like conditions of March. That's when most plants will bloom, heralding the start of our honey season. The second rainy season generally coincides with our hurricane season, June to November. August to November are the wettest months, a condition which works against the bees because it washes away any nectar that is present in the flowers.

At school, I got lost in the study of bees, learning about how they support our ecosystems and about bee by-products like propolis, bee-bread, and royal jelly. These natural and powerful medicinal and dietary supplements were truly mind-blowing. Learning about all of this was a galvanizing moment for me as a teenager. My interest in the relationship between nature and agriculture was aroused, and those early experiences catapulted my entry into the world of agriculture.

My other major interest in school was history. My history teacher at CCSS was Mr. Clyde P. Vincent. He was a critical person in my life. He was very clear in his teaching—he was frank. During a time of great change for me, moving to the city from the countryside and every-thing else, I appreciated this clarity. He would say things like, "I'm not here to teach you, but I can guide you and support you." These types of comments really helped me to understand that education was not something I could receive from my teachers; ultimately, I had to teach myself. But the guidance of people like Mr. Vincent was instrumental in helping me reach this understanding.

I graduated in 1989, and to my great pleasure, I won the prize for agriculture—a scientific calculator.

My first agricultural science teacher at CCSS, Mr. Octavian Charles (a.k.a. "Patch"), had a big impact in motivating me to pursue agriculture. At some point, he encouraged me to look into a post-secondary program at the Guyana School of Agriculture. In a few years I would leave St. Lucia to attend this school and begin the next stage of my lifelong fascination with agriculture. But before that, I found myself back at the primary school in La Ressource that I had left so many years earlier.

My interest in history was different than my interest in agriculture, which played such a big role in my day-to-day life. History was more of an intellectual pursuit than a practical one: it wouldn't really contribute to my career (or so I thought). But I had a curious mind and a keen interest in the past. My early impression of history was that it was purely an academic interest. I thought that Caribbean history existed only in the past and that it should and must remain there.

It was only many years later, when I was on the farm worker program in Canada, that I would realize how alive history was in the present and how deeply intertwined it was with agriculture. In particular, I began to notice the echoes of slavery, indentured labour, and colonialism in my experiences as a migrant farm worker. These reflections were critical in eventually pushing me to speak out against the injustices of Canada's farm labour system. So it was in Canada that my long-time interests in history and agriculture would unexpectedly come together in a powerful way for me.

Chapter 5
TEACHING AND LEARNING

I graduated from CCSS in 1989 and immediately began job hunting. In this period, St. Lucia's economy was doing very well, the population was growing, and so the government was building more schools. Teachers were thus in high demand, and I got a job as a primary school teacher at my former school, La Ressource. I taught standard two, which would be ten- or eleven-year-olds. I was filling in for a maternity leave, so I was only there for one year.

In years gone by, most of the teachers at La Ressource were from outside of the community. So now to have somebody from the community—a graduate of the school—be a teacher was significant. As a teacher, you mentor a lot in the community. And people regarded me very highly, which was a strange experience for an eighteen-year-old fresh out of secondary school. Of course, the pay did not reflect the stature given to teachers. Still, it was much better than the pay available to people with only a primary school education.

Teaching was not easy, especially because I had no training to be an educator. It felt like I'd been a passenger all my life, and suddenly I was asked to be the driver. Really, I was more of a student than a teacher, and it is not an exaggeration to say that I learned more than the children!

I ended up learning a lot of things. For the first time, all the skills that I had learned in life—and mostly was not even aware of—were now being tested and improved upon.

There were all sorts of questions that I had to find answers to on the fly. How do you manage a large group of children? How do you keep a group engaged when there are pupils at different levels? How do you deal with talkative, active, and quiet children, all in the same classroom?

It was a great challenge for me to simplify secondary school-level concepts to a level that these children could understand. It took me some time to get comfortable with doing this. I had a lot of support here from my colleague and mentor Mrs. Clarabelle N. "Myrna" Clarke and the school principal Ms. Catherine "Sayleetar" Francis; they were very patient in helping me to simplify my lessons and present them in a way that made teaching and learning fun. Sayleetar was a captivating and mesmerizing storyteller. She had a knack for getting and keeping her audience laser-focused during her classes. She was able to stimulate every sensory organ during her lessons.

Teaching at La Ressource also gave me a new perspective on the problems of poverty and illiteracy in St. Lucia. Soon after I started working there, the principal told me that the school had the lowest attendance in the whole island. The reason was that there were so many children who would be taken away from school to help on the farm, especially on harvest days when more hands were needed. The magnitude of this problem really struck me.

An important piece of context here is that, in the mid-twentieth century, agriculture in St. Lucia changed from being dominated by sugar cane to being dominated by bananas.[25] Whereas with sugar cane, there is one harvest for the year and one income, with bananas, farmers can harvest throughout the year, meaning that their cash flow is much more evenly distributed.

Another important development in this period was that, for the first time, the average person had relatively easy access to credit. This was an economic revolution. It brought about a significant improvement in people's standard of living, the biggest yardstick being the switch from houses with thatched roofs to ones with galvanized zinc roofs.

But there was also a negative side to this revolution. It was after this economic transformation took hold that children began to be taken away from school to help on the farm. The children observed a couple of things during that time: one, that their parents didn't have an education, and two, that their parents could easily access credit from banks and cooperatives. They began to reason, I don't need an education, so what's the point of having an education when I can have a decent standard of living? During these boom times, the old, golden formula for success—go to school, work hard, get a good job, retire happy—no longer made sense to the children and it was thrown out the window.

So green gold did a lot of harm in the sense that the children did not see the importance of having an education. They witnessed that even though their parents did not have one, they could still access credit and climb the economic ladder.

Of course, not all families were able to climb that ladder, and as a teacher I frequently came face to face with students' poverty. I would see some children dressed very shabbily, coming to school without breakfast, not having access to proper nutrition at home. And the schools did not provide any meals, meaning that these children might not eat until after midday. The instability of these children's lives was also reflected in their inconsistent attendance, missing school or not returning after lunch. They were often without textbooks or school supplies, another result of their poverty.

All of this was an eye opener for me. Seeing it from the perspective of a teacher gave me new insights on where St. Lucia's high rates of illiteracy came from and on how poverty and economic circumstances limited people's access to a good education. Another thing that became clear to me was how chronically underfunded our schools were. As just one example, there was no library in the school at the time I was there. In fact, there was no library in the entire Mabouya Valley. In order to get a set of encyclopedias for the school, in 1989–90, teachers and parents had to fundraise. When we finally purchased the encyclopedias, it was a big success. That made us feel good, and they were a great resource for the students, but it also shows the type of situation we were dealing with. With so little funding for public education, it was not surprising that literacy rates were so low.

The most special thing about being a teacher was the strong relationships I was able to build with the children. I'm not sure how much of an impact I had on them, but to this day, when my former students see me, they greet me with warmth and enthusiasm, which makes me feel like I did have some positive influence in their lives. They greet me like a friend, reminding me of Socrates's observation, Who can I teach but a friend? This reflects a big shift in teaching styles from my days as a student, when teachers carried a big stick, so to speak.

◇◇◇

After my year teaching at La Ressource, I taught on and off over the years at three different schools, for about ten years in total. One was in

Mabouya Valley, one was in Dennery Village (my former school, DJSS), and one in Cul de Sac, near Castries. My last teaching appointment was around 2001–2002.

But in a way, I've never stopped being a teacher. While working in Canada on the farm worker program, I quickly realized that many of my co-workers had very low literacy levels. Truly, my level of formal education made me quite unusual within the program. So I would help them with things like explaining letters from the government about social insurance cards or child tax benefits, or with their spelling when sending important messages, or with using various apps on their phones. A Jamaican co-worker began calling me "Teacher," and the nickname stuck among a number of my colleagues on the farm.

Chapter 6
GUYANA

Two years after graduating secondary school, my love for agriculture and desire to qualify for better-paying jobs pushed me to further pursue my education. Taking advantage of a modest student loan from the St. Lucia Development Bank (a government-created corporation), in 1991 I travelled to Guyana to pursue a diploma in general agriculture at the Guyana School of Agriculture, in the capital city, Georgetown.

This was my first time leaving St. Lucia and my first time travelling in an airplane, which touched down in Trinidad and Tobago before continuing on to Guyana after a long day of travel. I learned a lot from being in a new environment and comparing it with my home country. Guyana is a vast country, with large parts of its inhabited coastal areas lying below sea level and flat as a pancake. This was a big contrast to tiny, mountainous St. Lucia. Georgetown was so flat that a family of three could travel around town on a bicycle without any difficulty. Horse-drawn carts were also a common sight. Both of these modes of transportation were quite unusual to me.

I was also struck by the fact that tertiary, or post-secondary, education in Guyana was completely free to citizens of that country. I noticed as well that the rate of illiteracy was much lower than in St. Lucia. These were the results of more progressive social policies in Guyana.

Like in St. Lucia, Guyana's people descend from both Africans and Indians, but the latter make up a much bigger share of the population, with the country split roughly fifty-fifty between people of African and Indian heritage. The differences between St. Lucia and Guyana really came into focus for me with religion. Indian worship sites were very obvious in Guyana, a big difference from my home country. There were also a much greater number of churches from other Christian denominations than in St. Lucia.

But another sort of religion was shared in common between the two places. Just like in St. Lucia, cricket was the main sport and a unifying force in Guyana.

Being in Guyana was the first time that I really realized that I could speak a second language. When I would speak in Creole with other St. Lucians, other people could not understand. In St. Lucia, Creole was, at that time, considered to be backward. But those same prejudices did not exist in Guyana, and I gained a new appreciation for my bilingual upbringing.

When I arrived in Guyana in 1991, the country was in a period of transition away from the authoritarianism and economic chaos of the later years of Forbes Burnham's presidency. Burnham was Guyana's chief political leader—first as prime minister and then as president after a change in the country's system of government—from 1964 to 1985. Burnham, who had declared Guyana socialist, had no tolerance for opposition, especially towards the end of his regime. In 1980, for example, Dr. Walter Rodney—a radical, charismatic intellectual and political figure who had challenged the government—was assassinated by a car bomb in what is widely agreed to have been a state-ordered assassination. (My stay in Guyana was the first time that I was introduced to Dr. Rodney's teachings, which informed my political education and continue to shape my understanding of the world to this day—especially his emphasis on using knowledge to challenge oppression.)

Burnham also instituted economic reforms—including trade restrictions—that had disastrous effects on the national economy. After Burnham died in 1985, Desmond Hoyte took over as president, and at the time I arrived in the country, he was bringing in reforms that were moving Guyana towards more democratic elections and liberal economic policies. Before I departed for Guyana, I had been told to pack many basic staples like powdered milk, since there was a ban on the importation of goods. But when I got there, I found this was not necessary, since the trade doors had already opened and goods were coming in.

But signs of the country's recent economic struggles were everywhere. I found that there was a lot of infrastructure in place but that it was in a state of disrepair. This was on display at my school as well. For example, the school had a number of tractors, but most of them were out of service. Other vehicles and equipment on campus were also in bad shape. The school buildings sorely needed a new coat of paint and generally were not in the best condition. In essence, the school was lacking in resources. There was no computer lab. It did have microscopes, but they were woefully out of date.

The Guyana School of Agriculture had previously attracted students from all over the Caribbean and even from Africa. But by the time I attended, its reputation had somewhat diminished. There were still foreign students—ten of us from St. Lucia and five Grenadians in my year—but not as many as before. By the time I arrived in Guyana, the School of Agriculture's neighbouring school (Regional Educational Programme for Animal Health Assistants, or REPAHA) attracted far more students from the English-speaking Caribbean.

I did not find the general agriculture program to be very progressive. A lot of the material was outdated and did not reflect contemporary agricultural practices. There were many basic but essential skills—such as plant grafting or animal castration—that we simply did not learn.

Though the program was a bit disappointing, I still got a lot out of the experience. For one, I made some great friends, especially with the students from Grenada: Moses Frank, Trevor Thompson, Desmond Isaac, Cecil McQueen, and Francis Mahon. We bonded in two main areas. The first was over food. We lived in a dormitory on campus and at first had our meals at the canteen. But the food was not to our liking. We joked that the menu was rice and peas today, and tomorrow peas with rice. So we began to cook for ourselves, and since I had a bit of experience cooking from when I was growing up, I became the main chef, and cooking and eating together became a bonding experience.

I also was able to help my Grenadian friends with math. Mathematics has always been my strong point. The professor who taught us mathematics in Guyana was very jovial, but also very fast in his teaching. For me, it was more his jokes that kept me in class than anything else. Students struggled to keep up with the pace at which he would write formulas and examples on the board. Since I was good at math, I was still able to catch most of the concepts, but many of my friends really struggled. So I was happy to tutor them in our dorm.

I later realized that when I was helping to tutor my friends, they were also really helping me. In order to explain the concepts to them, I had to first understand them sufficiently myself. So I came to realize that by the time I had finished tutoring my friends and gone off to study on my own, I no longer had any reason to study, because I had already understood the concept and mastered it enough that I could explain it. I ended up finishing the program with distinction and the highest average in my cohort, and I am convinced that tutoring my friends played a big role in this. I thought I was helping them, but they were helping me too.

My studies in Guyana also helped advance my career when I returned to St. Lucia, where over the years, I worked a number of jobs related to agriculture.

◇◇◇

A final note about my time in Guyana is that it was one of the earliest times that I gained some awareness of the two faces of Canada on the world stage. My five Grenadian friends in the program were all on scholarships from CIDA, the Canadian government's international development agency. Through their scholarships, my Grenadian friends brought Canada directly into my life. Using their monthly stipends, they purchased all the culturally appropriate foods that we cooked. They literally covered all my food while I helped tutor them. Canada's role in helping them finance their education—and by extension mine too—is the sort of thing that the country prides itself on.

But I also learned about a more sinister side of Canada in Guyana. There was a big gold-mining operation called Omai that was owned and operated by a Canadian company. During my time in Guyana, in the early 1990s, there was a big controversy when mercury escaped from the mine and seeped into nearby waterways, posing a serious threat to local communities and the country in general. Then, a couple years after I left Guyana, I remember hearing about the collapse of a tailings dam in 1995 that resulted in about three million cubic metres of cyanide-tainted waste gushing into the Essequibo River, devastating plant and animal life as well as many Indigenous communities along the river.[26] This was an early red flag about Canada for me.

Chapter 7

WORK, FAMILY, AND COMMUNITY

After I returned from Guyana in 1993, I worked a few different jobs related to agriculture, in both public and private sectors, benefiting from the strong local economy. At first, I returned to the classroom as an agricultural science teacher at George Charles Secondary School, in Cul de Sac Valley, close to Castries.

After a year of teaching, I secured a position with the Ministry of Agriculture as an agricultural extension officer, where my job was to help rehabilitate the banana industry after tropical storm Debby, which struck in 1994. I travelled around the Mabouya Valley, meeting with banana farmers and providing various forms of support: facilitating an incentive program that paid farmers to build drainage in their fields, and providing young banana plants (suckers) for planting as well as agricultural inputs such as fertilizers and pesticides. I also organized and led educational sessions on various aspects of banana produc-tion—everything from soil fertility to pesticide safety. The position of extension officer came with a travelling allowance, which allowed me to buy my first vehicle, a used yellow Toyota Hilux pickup truck.

At the end of this two-year contract, I returned to the classroom, teaching agricultural science for three more years at George Charles, followed by one year at a different school, Dennery Junior Secondary School. In 2002, I got another opportunity in the public sector—this time as a port quarantine officer, a better-paying job than teaching and one that included a transportation budget. In this position, I worked alongside customs officers to prevent the entrance of foreign pests and disease at the Castries airport and seaport. (I alternated between each port on a weekly basis.) Like the extension officer job, this was just a two-year contract, as was common for positions in the public service at this time: St. Lucia was following the economic line of the International Monetary Fund and tightening the belt on government expenditures. So after my two years as a quarantine officer, I was on the job hunt yet again.

This time, I got a position in the private sector, working for a bank as an agricultural credit officer. My job was to process credit applications from farmers. Unlike the contract work I had done for the government, this job was permanent and full-time. I stayed in this position for five years before leaving for self-employment in 2009, as I'll describe in the next chapter.

◇◇◇

Coming back to the mid-1990s, when I was newly returned from Guyana, in September 1994, St. Lucia was dealt a mighty blow by tropical storm Debby, a major storm that brought down the banana crop with it. A tropical storm is one grade below a hurricane in intensity, and tropical storm Debby will forever be remembered for extensive flooding and countless landslides.

At that time, I was living with my mom. But shortly after Debby hit, I decided to move in with my father, who was by then eighty-three years old, because I noticed he was struggling to take care of himself while living alone. In St. Lucia, we have very few nursing homes, and in the countryside it is not very common for elderly people to live in nursing or retirement homes. I'm not sure if it's due to culture or cost, but elderly people are usually cared for by their families.

Living with my father, there was no electricity and no indoor bathroom; instead, we had an outhouse (or as we call it in St. Lucia, a pit toilet). There was a two-burner tabletop gas stove in the house, but we also used wood fuel outside. On rainy days we would use the stove inside, but on sunny days we would use the wood fuel outside. This meant that we spent a lot of time outdoors, where we were at the mercy of the sun flies, especially in the early morning and early evening.

The sun flies were a real nuisance to me. To get away from the flies and also to spend time with friends, I would often go in the evenings to Belmont to the cricket club I belonged to, the Young Generation Sports Club. Here I would practise cricket, attend club meetings, and see my friends. The over an hour long walk did not bother me.

Being so young, with no prior experience of caring for an elderly person, I didn't know what I was walking into. My father and I had a fundamental misunderstanding about how our living arrangement would work. He wasn't too happy with my constant outings to Belmont and my coming home late, since it meant that he had no company in the evening time. When I first arrived to live with him, I made it clear to my father that if he needed anything, to just let me know. But he expected me to offer him help without prompting. Obviously, I had no experience living with an elderly person. I only came to better understand this miscommunication later in life.

One day, my sister who lives in the northern part of the island decided to take our father to spend a weekend with her and her family. A weekend turned to a week, a week turned into a month, one month turned into several, and months turned into years. My father ended up living with my sister until he died in June of 1998. This meant that I was left alone in my father's house.

Now that I was living alone I could go to Belmont even more and stay out as long as I wanted before returning. I wanted to spend as much time as possible with my friends before returning to the empty house. Eventually my friends at the club began to take notice and invited me to sleep over at their houses. I gladly took up their invitations and was much happier as a result.

Spending more time at the sports club in Belmont led me to take on a greater role within the community. Around this time, Victor "Black" Edwin, a member of the club executive committee, approached me about becoming president. It was a position that no one seemed to want. I was taken aback at first and did not give him an answer right away. Over the next few days, a barrage of club members approached me one-on-one and urged me to take the position. I was not expecting that. In the end, I succumbed to their demand and was named president.

This was the first time I had ever served on the executive of a committee, and I still remember the rush of seeing my name associated with the position of president. A highlight of my time as president was when the club travelled to neighbouring French Martinique for the first time to participate in an exchange. This endeared me to club members, who saw this initiative as a big step forward for the club. To this day, a few people from the community greet me as "Prezzy."

Looking back, I am so thankful to all the club members, Mitchel Boodhoo, Michael "Isaac" Rampal, Daniel "Tarbac" Sandiford, Lucas "Lulu" Sandiford, Andre Chastenet, Linus St. Juste, Bachus Olice, Randy and Peter St. Ange, and others, for pulling me into that role. That experience of serving on the executive of the club whetted my appetite for more volunteering and community building.

I was also heartily encouraged in this direction by Patrick "Slinger" Velinor. Slinger was a few years older than me, a young leader in the local Catholic Church and Mabouya Valley community. At one point during this period, he pulled me aside and told me that he saw some skills in me that could really benefit the community, and he encouraged me to get more involved. Coming from someone I looked up to, this made a big impression on me.

In the years to come, I would work alongside Peace Corps volunteers through my role as a member of the Belmont Development Committee executive. I also served on the executive committees of the Dennery Cricket Club, La Ressource (now Mabouya Valley) Cooperative Credit Union, Mille Fleurs Honey Producers Cooperative, Mabouya Valley Development Committee, and Dennery Valley Minibus Association. By volunteering with these different groups, I developed the confidence to become an enumerator for a few national surveys within my community, such as the National Population and Housing Census, National Adult Literacy Survey, National Abattoir Survey, and Belmont Development Community Survey. The last of these was part of the European Union–funded Poverty Reduction through Community-Based Development Planning project.

I thought I was just volunteering. I had no idea that these experiences, which enabled me to see the stark inequality and injustices within my community—everything from the sharp differences in the quality of education between city and countryside, to government inaction in the face of widespread poverty and its social effects—would politicize me. Little did I know that volunteering in my community in St. Lucia would end up being just a precursor to my eventual destination of becoming an activist in Canada.

◇◇◇

It was during these days and nights spent in Belmont that I first met the very attractive woman who would become my significant other and the mother of my children, Diana. We first got together sometime around 1996. Diana was very quiet, gentle, and easygoing. She never made much of a fuss about anything. But though she was quiet, Diana was not shy. She loved social activities like going to clubs and dancing. I always found it ironic that somebody so quiet would like something so noisy and social. I did not enjoy these same things, which became an area of conflict later on. But early on in our relationship, it didn't bother me. As they say, love is blind.

Our first child was born on March 30, 1998, shortly before my father passed. We named him Gania, combining the first two letters from my name with letters from Diana's name.

Very soon after Gania was born, we began to have trouble in our relationship. As I mentioned, our different social lives caused conflict. I tried to please her by going to clubs, but for me, it was like being a fish out of water. We separated soon after we had our son, but later got back together.

Diana gave birth to our second child, a girl named Christi, on June 22, 2000, two years to the month of my father's passing.

But the difficulties in our relationship soon resurfaced. Beyond the question of socializing, we also fought over the baptism of our children. In St. Lucia, it was standard practice to christen a child in the Catholic Church. I had been an altar boy growing up, but as I entered my teenage years, I began to see the church more critically: as an agent of social control and as upholding the political status quo. Studying Caribbean history and learning about the role of the church in colonialism—Christianity was, of course, one of the three Cs of colonialism—was crucial to reaching this new understanding. As I came to these conclusions, I began to attend mass less regularly, and by the time I was twenty I had stopped altogether. So when my children were born, neither one was baptized or raised Catholic. Diana was not happy with this, and it was another area of conflict.

Before my daughter turned one, we separated again, this time for good. We decided that my son, Gania, would live with me, while Christi would stay with her mother. We also decided that the children would spend every weekend together, alternating weekends between Diana and me.

I had many financial challenges in raising my son. I had student loans, car payments, and other expenses. Combined with the fact that

Diana did not have any income and the lack of a social safety net in St. Lucia, it was difficult to make ends meet, ensure a quality education, and provide the sorts of material things—a bicycle, for example—that I would have liked to provide for my children.

Diana died on International Women's Day, March 8, 2005, after battling cancer for a year or so. On her deathbed she asked that Christi, who would soon turn five, be raised by Diana's sister. I agreed to this request, though later in life I came to regret it.

◇◇◇

Just like my mother had done for me, I encouraged Gania in his education. I made an effort to read to my son at night. In one book that I remember reading with him, near the beginning, there were pictures of the book's characters with their names underneath. Later in the book, the pictures alone would appear, and I would ask him, "Who's that?" It was so amazing: I couldn't even keep up with the names, but he was able to. That was really striking. A child's mind is like a sponge; they absorb things so easily.

On the weekends that both children were with me, one thing we really enjoyed doing was going to the beach. We would often go with a group of friends and their children. Some of my friends would go fishing or catch crabs, but I would be the "fire guy," meaning that I was responsible for cooking the food. My children enjoyed playing with the other kids in the sand on the seashore. And we all enjoyed cooking, eating, and spending the day together.

◇◇◇

It was extremely difficult for my children not to have their mother in their lives growing up. As the old saying goes, nobody can replace the love of a mother. And for Christi, being raised by her aunt also meant that she was separated from me, even more so when I began to work in the farm worker program.

Indeed, out of the many problems migrant workers face, being separated from family is the most crushing. Each year that I was in the program, as my travel date to Canada approached, the pain of leaving my children caused me to seriously question whether I should keep participating in the program. Ultimately my desire to provide for them would win out.

WORKING THE LAND

I was born and raised in the countryside. Agriculture has always been my passion. I live it, I see it, I breathe it, I sleep in it, I dream it.

My father was a beekeeper, a mixed farmer, and a carpenter. He did several things, but a lot of them were related to agriculture. Even with his carpentry jobs, many of the people who hired him were farmers. Whenever agriculture did well, I could tell, because farmers would hire my father to do carpentry work to improve their homes. And in the countryside, your life can never improve if agriculture—which is the backbone of the community—does not do well.

By 2009, four years after Diana's death, I had become, like my father before me, an entrepreneur engaged in multiple lines of work, all connected in one way or another to agriculture. After building up some of my lines of business on the side for a few years, in 2009 I decided to quit my job as an agricultural credit officer and devote myself full-time to my business. This was the first time that I had ever been self-employed, and it was very different from having a regular job, as I had for the previous decade and a half. With the knowledge and experience of working in both the public and private sectors, for the first time I felt the great sense of freedom that comes with being able to control my own time.

I had five different lines of work, and I took great comfort in knowing that my income was diversified. At that point in time, I felt that I had freedom in terms of both time and money. It was a rare feeling of serenity in my life.

What were the five things I was doing?

One, I was operating a very small greenhouse, maybe thirty by sixty feet. By St. Lucian standards, that is a decent size, but compared to the mega-greenhouse operations of Leamington, it would be no more than a dot. Still, that one greenhouse was able to generate income. My main crop was cucumbers, which were exported to the United Kingdom through a contact of mine who had a marketing arrangement not only for cucumbers but for a variety of crops, including breadfruit, plantains, mangoes, soursop, golden apples, and others.

Second was beekeeping, which I had learned and inherited from my father. This was my longest-standing entrepreneurial activity, which I had been doing on the side of my day job since the mid-1990s.

Third, for the first time in my life, I was a shopkeeper, operating what in Canada would be called a convenience store. This, too, was connected to agriculture, since my customers were all dependent on agriculture for their livelihoods.

Fourth, I was a middleman, meaning that I would buy produce from farmers—mostly bananas and plantains—and sell it to somebody who took care of the marketing. Being a middleman meant maintaining relationships with the farmers. I would provide them with empty boxes for packing their harvested fruits, they would provide me with the produce, and I would pay them—all on a weekly basis.

The fifth thing I was doing was supplying inputs to farmers, especially fertilizer.

◇◇◇

Beekeeping was especially important to me. It represented both the beauty and challenges of agriculture. Beekeeping was always a part of my family's tradition. My father kept bees on a semi-commercial level for over sixty years, until I took over his operation in 1995–96. His carpentry skills came in handy in building his bee boxes and the frames that went inside them.

In two consecutive years in the 1980s, my father won first prize in his category in an annual national agricultural exhibition at the Vieux Fort Secondary School. Both times, I was a part of my family's contingent that manned our exhibits. Mr. Peter Vidal, an agricultural and forestry officer, played a great role in encouraging my father to participate in the exhibition. Mr. Vidal went above and beyond by providing assistance to transport our exhibits to and from the fair. Our exhibits showed a sample of all the basic tools and equipment used in beekeeping, such as hive tool, smoker, bee brush, bee box, honey extractor, queen excluder, bottom board, hive cover, wired honey frames, wax foundations, coveralls, veil, rubber gloves, and hard hat. The centre of attraction was a mini-hive, a carefully designed wood and glass structure, with a queen bee trapped in a smaller glass case. People attending the exhibition were always blown away to see a queen bee so up close. My father once again put his mastery of carpentry to use to build the mini-hive.

My father claimed that it was costing us too much to travel to the exhibition and cover two days of meals and refreshment, expenses that were much greater than the prize money he received. In addition, any time spent travelling to the exhibition was time away from his business, always a concern for a small business owner. But to my liking, Mr. Vidal was always able to convince him otherwise. I was happy to accompany my father to the exhibition, because those rare and precious moments gave me a welcome break from home chores and took me to new places. I also got to know and understand my father better in a different social environment. Our exhibit station would be over-crowded with curious people from all walks of life. Meeting so many new people broadened my horizons.

Beekeeping contributed to my father's popularity in the community and around the island. The value of honey in traditional medicine was well known, and he was among the few people who knew the art of producing it.

My first set of encounters with bees was a rude awakening for me. There was always a shortage of coveralls and protective equipment for onlookers and children like me. So I was often stung as my father tended to the hives. Beekeeping was the first experience to teach me that difficult roads sometimes lead to beautiful destinations.

The swelling and accompanying pain around my eyes, fingers, and other parts of my body from all those bee stings were so agonizing that I convinced myself that I would settle for any occupation but beekeeping. I held that mindset for a very long time. I even carried it into that crucial stretch of time when my role changed from spectator to player. As I got older, I was given the opportunity to help out with the work in the apiary, dressed in coveralls and equipped with all the protective gear that was available. None of that boosted my confidence. There was never a day that I did not get a bee sting. Yes, my face was now covered with a veil, but the bees always found a way to reach my skin to sting me. The stings on my fingers, especially near my fingernails, were the most painful.

With time, as my father got older and less able-bodied, my role in the hives grew bigger, as did the expectations of me. This process was hastened when Francis, better known as "Seekoye," my second brother on my mom's side, and the next in line to take over from my father, suddenly passed away in 1990. At that moment, I made the decision to drop my old negative mindset and to take on a new and more empowering one. It was a total mind shift and a powerful turning point in my life. I decided to work without any protective rubber gloves, which gave reasonable protection to my fingers from bee stings but were too cumbersome for me and rendered me inefficient. Working in the hives without gloves meant that I would be stung more often—not something that gets less painful over time. To this day, this decision represents a golden milestone and a permanent reference point in my life. I felt like I had reached a beautiful mental destination. Beekeeping helped me to confront a fear I had in my mind and to take my power back from something I had given power over me. That one invisible but mammoth mental step cemented my passion for agriculture.

Beekeeping brought other benefits to my life as well. In doing my own marketing, I created and built my own network and developed great relationships both in and out of St. Lucia that have lasted to this very day.

One special friendship was with a young man named Kade "Parry" Theodule, who I had hired as a part-time worker to help me on honey harvesting days. I thought I had hired a part-time worker, but it turned out that he saw me playing the role of a father. He used his income from helping me to complete his secondary school education. Today he is happily married with three kids, living in New York City, where he works as a painter. His second child, Kayla, is my number one fan in New York. Whenever we speak, he reminds me that his home is my home.

Beekeeping was also great for me financially, for a few years in the late 1990s. As a beekeeper, I had the most non-perishable natural farm product, in constant high demand. My income was diversified, as I also had a steady day job as a teacher during those years. I had a cash flow that allowed me to save. Those were the best financial days of my life.

But those boom times did not last forever. In the year 2000, my hives were infested with varroa mites, a parasite that attacks honeybees. Varroa mite, a foreign pest which was only introduced to St. Lucia in 1998, is known to destroy between 50 to 100 percent of infected hives.[27] I lost over 90 percent of my hives in a very short space of time. Many other beekeepers in St. Lucia faced similar levels of destruction. The introduction of this exotic pest to St. Lucia came as a total surprise. Effective methods of controlling varroa mite do exist, but they take some time to implement; we were caught off guard and were unprepared to deal with it. In fact, it took St. Lucian beekeepers a very long time to figure it out, as it worked its way down the island from the north. The mite came very close to taking me out of production and driving me out of the market entirely. So by 2009, beekeeping was, in financial terms, the smallest of my five entrepreneurial activities, even though it still had a great deal of personal meaning to me.

The other aspects of my livelihood also faced challenges related to pests. Specifically, in early 2010, St. Lucia's banana farmers began to experience an infestation of a disease we had never had before: Black Sigatoka. Black Sigatoka is a fungal disease that leaves black marks on the leaves of banana trees and can cut their fruit production by as much as 50 percent. Whereas plant diseases we had dealt with before, such as Cordana leaf spot, were relatively cheap to manage, it was extremely costly to treat banana trees for Black Sigatoka. So once this disease began to take hold, the returns that the farmers were getting after they paid out the cost of pests and disease control were really discouraging. The economic harm caused by Black Sigatoka also affected me, since struggling farmers had less to spend on inputs or goods from my shop, and the smaller crops meant a reduction in my transactions as a middleman.

◇◇◇

Black Sigatoka placed additional stress on a sector that was already in steady decline, ever since the 1997 ruling by the World Trade Organization (WTO) that ended Caribbean countries' preferential access to European markets for banana exports. The United States had brought a complaint to the WTO, protesting the protected market share that European countries had granted their former colonies in the Caribbean, claiming it was a violation of the principles of free trade.[28] This ruling caused a great deal of harm in St. Lucia and elsewhere in the Caribbean. The WTO is one of many institutions that systematically destabilize the Global South.[29]

As the banana sector declined, tourism took its place as St. Lucia's main economic driver. By 2007, nearly a million visitors were arriving yearly in St. Lucia, about 60 percent of them cruise ship passengers.[30] But tourism didn't offer a lot of stability either. The global economic crisis of 2008–2009 resulted in a sharp downturn in tourism, damaging St. Lucia's economy even further.

By mid-2010, then, St. Lucia was facing a difficult economic situation, one that was also affecting my own livelihood. But these challenges would pale in comparison to what came next.

Chapter 9

THE HURRICANE

E xactly one year after I took that bold step to be self-employed, everything changed for me and for many St. Lucians, in late October 2010, when the island was struck by hurricane Tomas.

In school, we were taught that the hurricane season starts from the first of June to the thirtieth of November. It was drilled into us in a way that we could never forget: "June, too soon. July, stand by. August is a must. September is a month to remember. October, it's not over. November, it's all over." It was a fun rhyme to learn, but the reality of experiencing hurricanes was anything but fun.

Hurricanes and tropical storms had been a part of my life since childhood. The first big storm I can remember was hurricane Allen, which struck St. Lucia when I was nine years old, in 1980—just one year after independence. From my experience with storms making landfall in St. Lucia, I've made two observations. One, these large storms always seem to hit us when farms are in good shape and production is looking up. And two, most damage is inflicted during the night.

Tomas was slow in approaching St. Lucia. Throughout the day of October 30 it was very rainy and windy. That day I was at the shop and my sales were very unusual. I was busier than usual as residents from the community came to stock up on essentials, such as candles, matches, salt, sugar, non-perishables like rice, canned foods, salted crackers, bottled water, and so on. Almost everyone who came in to patronize freely and willingly shared their stories, experiences, and fears of what was to come.

Just like I was accustomed to, the worst part of the hurricane, with its heavy rainfall, came at night. Because of the inclement weather and flooded roads and bridges, I was forced to spend the night in the shop.

My children were in separate homes at the time of the hurricane. My daughter was living with her aunt, and my son was with my neighbour in Dennery. .

During the night, no one went to bed. Everyone stayed up and kept a vigil. Those who tried to get some rest were prevented by the strong winds of the hurricane. The winds came in waves of high velocity followed by brief periods of calm. The intense periods were marked by banging, clanging, deafening noise as partially secured metal objects were blown around. We were also kept awake by the wind blowing rainwater into our homes as very fine mist.

The winds inflicted damage in a manner that seemed very systematic. The weaker objects were knocked out or blown away first: the snapping of bananas and plantains, breaking of branches, toppling of trees, blowing down of pit toilets and loose objects that were not properly secured.

During the night, people knocked on the shop door to report on their damage. Everyone was checking on each other. That's how the Belmont community is: tightly knit.

I wasn't too worried about myself. Fortunately, the shop was sheltered and protected from the full force of the hurricane winds by a mid-sized brick building that served as a community centre. I also took comfort in knowing that my income was diversified. I believed that the shop was protected and would not be affected. With those thoughts dominating, I was totally oblivious to the extent that the damages inflicted by Tomas would impact me. Truly, I could not see the trouble that lay ahead.

In the morning the extent of the damage became clear. The first thing that I noticed after I stepped outside that morning—after it became obvious that it was calm, the winds had died down, and the hurricane had passed over—was that the place looked brighter and different. The trees and branches that previously blocked our view were all blown away. All of a sudden, places miles away that were previously hidden were now visible. The banana crop had been totally wiped out. The countless fresh red wounds on the hills and steep mountains created by landslides were eyesores.

Tomas's heavy rains caused lots of flooding and landslides, with the latter partially the result of the cut-and-burn method of cultivation that I've described. In a way, landslides are just a more dramatic type of soil erosion. These landslides compounded the problem of flooding. They not only brought down trees and vegetative materials that blocked the free flow of water in rivers, but the accompanying large volume of mud, stones, and silt were deposited all along the riverbeds. Raised riverbeds made the problem of flooding worse. It was a big mess. It took several weeks for the river waters and the nearby ocean to become clear from the turbidity caused by these landslides.

Literally every road in my community was blocked. Roads on the hillsides were made impassable by landslides and fallen trees. In the flat areas of the valley, the roads were either flooded or blocked with debris and trees pushed down by the flood waters. The main road to the city was blocked off completely from Tomazo, in Mabouya Valley, to Ravine Poison, in Cul de Sac Valley. That portion of the main road is all steep slopes of thick forest. It took several weeks to clear off all the massive landslides and fallen trees, meaning that the eastern side of the island was cut off from the city, where everything was centralized, for well over a month.

◇◇◇

Fortunately, my immediate and extended family all made it safely through the hurricane. In Belmont, not one roof was blown away and there were no reports of any deaths. Fourteen St. Lucians were not so lucky. For me and so many others, the damage of hurricane Tomas would be felt in the months and years ahead, as the full extent of its economic destruction became clear.

Tomas will forever be remembered for its high rainfall rather than the strong winds. The countless landslides and widespread flooding brought about by the rains associated with the very slow moving Tomas made it different from the typical hurricane. Worse yet, Tomas made landfall at a time when things were bad in the banana industry, delivering a near-deadly blow to the struggling sector. To this day, this is one of the most devastating parts of Tomas's legacy.

It took a couple of months for me to fully realize how much the storm would hurt my livelihood. After the storm, with the bananas, plantains, and other crops toppled, it was easy for people to get something to eat from those fallen trees. But that didn't last very long. After a couple of months, people did not have any source of income. The sales in my shop hit rock bottom. At that point, I realized that even though my income was diversified, it was not sustainable. The rug had been pulled out from under my feet. Even if I have a shop, that shop depends almost entirely on the world around it. My supplies came from the outside—namely, Castries. My customers came from the community. If those things suffer, the shop suffers. It took me a couple of months to realize that and the other effects.

It was these economic effects of the storm that eventually forced me to apply to the Canadian farm worker program.

I also see the storm in a bigger, geopolitical perspective. It is developed countries like Canada that have done the most to create the problem of climate change, which results in more frequent and severe hurricanes and storms. But it is developing countries that are paying a higher price for these "natural" disasters. And countries like Canada can even benefit from the fallout of these disasters, for example, by receiving climate migrants who are the backbone of their food production system—exactly what happened in my case.

Main road between Mabouya Valley and Castries, washed out by hurricane Tomas. Barre de Isle. Photo: Bill Mortley.

Harvesting Freedom

Chapter 10
JOINING THE FARM WORKER
PROGRAM

I t did not take very long before I started to feel the economic effects of the hurricane. My apiary and small greenhouse took a hard hit from the storm. Bananas and plantains were completely wiped away. My last option and only hope left was my shop. Not long after the hurricane I started recording a significant decline in daily sales. The shop was located in the small rural community of Belmont, where most of the residents were small farmers. The average farm is less than five acres, usually located on marginal hillside soils, with no irrigation or mechanization. Besides manual labour, which accounted for a large portion of farmers' high cost of production, the advent of Black Sigatoka ensured that net returns made banana production unprofitable for all the small producers. The heavy blow dealt to banana production by Black Sigatoka came in after the WTO ruling, which had an equally devastating effect.

Farming has always been a very risky undertaking. Devastation due to droughts and strong winds are common occurrences. Recovering from these natural events was generally manageable. But this time was different. Tomas made landfall at a time when banana production was not profitable. Most small farms were barely getting by, and many were being pushed out of business. Most of these small banana farmers had no crop insurance in place at a time when financial institutions were reluctant to extend credit to banana farmers.

The writing was on the wall for the future of the shop, which had all my hopes tied to it. This was an unprecedented time for me. I was caught off guard and unprepared to deal with it. This was the lowest point in my life, with a family to support and no source of income.

I moved from having five lines of business to zero. That was extremely difficult. I had a tough decision to make: whether to remain self-employed or seek employment.

I was deeply in love with the idea and the good feelings of time freedom that came with being self-employed. I did not think that I would ever have to give it up. But here I was, confronting it, only one year in. Everything seemed to conspire against my decision to remain self-employed. A whole chain of events, starting with the WTO ruling, had brought about the steady decline of the banana industry. This was followed by the global financial crisis that affected tourism and investments, contracting economies all over the world, especially in the Global South. The infestation of the varroa mite and Black Sigatoka in St. Lucia compounded a situation that was already bad. Tomas was the last nail in the coffin.

All of this led me to my predicament of whether to persist with self-employment (which was underemployment) or look for a job. But what were the options? They were very limited. I was staring desperation in the eye. The ground that I was standing on was no longer firm and solid. I felt I was drowning and was willing to do anything legal to generate income. I was being pushed by my discontents and simultaneously being pulled by my dreams. I had my ears on the ground for any employment opportunity. One such opportunity, and maybe the only opportunity, was to become a migrant farm worker, in what we commonly refer to as the Canadian farm program. (This would be the third time I inquired about joining the program. The first two times had been many years earlier, when I was around twenty years old, before I had even gone to Guyana, and my application had not moved forward.)

The requirements to join the program in 2011–12 were extremely easy for me:

1. Age: 22 to 44 (I was 40 at the time of application)
2. Farming or experience in agriculture (two reference letters required; no educational requirements)
3. Two character references from past teachers, pastors, etc.
4. Valid passport
5. Passport-size photos

6. Certificate of character (police background check)
7. Clean bill of health
8. Community background check

I applied at the Labour Department, in the capital, Castries. After several weeks, I was called to attend an in-person interview, which turned out to be a group interview for five applicants. One of the other applicants was a former student of mine, by that time in his twenties. It felt bad that I was competing with him. The official conducting the interview told us that they only needed two people out of the five. That was scary. For the duration of the interview that deflating fact occupied my whole brain. It took away all my enthusiasm and hope and instead ignited a strong sense of fear that lasted well beyond the duration of that interview up until I heard back from them. (I saw my former student again the night before I left for Canada and learned that he had not been accepted into the program. That made me feel uncomfortable all over again and dampened my optimism about going to Canada.)

Soon after the interview, roughly one year after Tomas, I received a phone call from the Labour Department telling me the extremely relieving news that I had been accepted into the program. Relieving because I was at the lowest point in my life financially and emotionally, with so much fear dominating my thoughts.

Initially I was in disbelief. That good news did not sink in not until the time I was given instructions on what needed to be done to prepare for my departure in mid-January. That was my watershed moment, that finally heralded the welcomed feeling of hope in my life. It felt like getting a drink of water after a long drought. At that moment, I wished I could place my life on pause. I wanted to stay in this frame of mind forever, even though I had no idea which province in Canada I was going to, nor the type of farm or work that I would be doing, and no hint of what the living and working conditions were.

Mentally, that remains one of my favourite moments. I think about it often, especially in moments when I'm faced with challenges. The fact that it took me three attempts to get in made this news and the feelings associated with it even more special to me.

To me, that news also carried some extra special meaning: You dream it, believe it, and achieve it. The three years that I spent at the

Canadian-funded Castries Comprehensive Secondary School was the time that the seed of thought and dream of being in Canada was planted.

◇◇◇

Everything comes at a price, though. I've never seen a rose flower without thorns. In St. Lucia it is a very common saying that if you love the rose you should expect the thorns. The first sign of thorns with the farm worker program came when I went back to the Labour Department to sign the paperwork. The official produced form after form, instructing me to "sign here, sign here, sign here," but never explained what I was signing or gave me any time to read it. This was a red flag, but I didn't let it dampen my enthusiasm. I was signing to join the program. The green light was on. I did the same thing as my colleagues in the program and just signed where they told me. We were so bent on pleasing the system because we wanted to protect our daily bread. Who were we to question things?

If I had been able to spend a bit more time studying the forms, I would have noticed some of the more troubling aspects of the program that I would come to know up close once I was working under the contract, aspects that I now refer to as the Twenty Injustices of Canada. For example, that I was forbidden from working for anyone other than my assigned employer, unless I received permission from the employer, the Eastern Caribbean liaison officer, and Human Resources and Skills Development Canada (the responsible federal department). Or that I was obligated to live in housing determined by my employer. Or that I was required to immediately return to St. Lucia at the end of my contract—good enough to work, but not good enough to stay, even if I had wanted to.

Not that reading any of these things more closely would have prevented me from signing the form. As I said, the green light was on. And given my desperate economic situation, I was not about to stand still and let it change to red.

The greatest price of being accepted to the farm worker program was that I would have to leave my children behind in St. Lucia. This was distressing. It also posed some logistical challenges, since I had to make sure that they would be in good hands while I was away. In the end, Christi remained with her aunt, while my sister Constance took care of Gania during my stint in Canada.

My next visit to the Labour Department was on the day before I was scheduled to depart for my first season in Canada, when I and fifteen other program participants were brought in for an orientation meeting with St. Lucian government officials. The deputy labour commissioner, the supervisor of the Labour Department, and their few support staff showed us a short DVD in a last-minute, unprepared manner at the very short orientation session. The video was supposed to prepare us for our season in Canada. Even though we would be arriving to Canada in January, the video never showed us how to dress. Instead it showed people of colour busily harvesting different crops out in the fields in the height of summer. You could see that the pace of work was fast. At the end of the orientation session, the officials told us to make sure that we did our best because we were ambassadors. We were representing our country. That was the teaching that they left us with.

The Labour Department took care of all the paperwork, including securing our travel visas from the nearest Canadian consulate (which in 2011 was in Trinidad and Tobago) and coordinating all our travel. Orientation ended with a reminder of our travel itinerary to Canada via Barbados, which started with our early-morning flight out of St. Lucia at the George F. L. Charles Airport in Castries. That meant leaving my home extremely early under the cover of darkness, something new and different to me. This I didn't mind, because I was embarking on a new journey filled with uncertainties.

As I boarded the flight that day in January 2012, in some ways I was simply taking the next steps of a journey I had been on for a long time, continuing my curious exploration of the vast world of agriculture and finding new ways to pursue my passion. But in another way, that step onto the plane was a departure, the first step into a completely different world and way of living than what I had known before. I boarded the plane with a particular idea about what Canada was and what my experience on the farm worker program might be like. By the time I got back on a plane to fly home, eight months later, those ideas had been completely shattered.

Part Two
A MIGRANT FARM WORKER

Chapter 11

WORKING IN THE GREENHOUSE

I *worked on the farm where I lived.*

The morning after the long, cold night that was my welcome to Canada, I found myself at a greenhouse in Leamington, at the southwestern tip of Ontario, fifty kilometres from the Windsor-Detroit border. For the first time, I came face to face with intensive agriculture being carried out over an extensive area.

The size, layout, and height of the greenhouse was mind-blowing to me. The greenhouse was the size of many football fields. The size and design reminded me of an estate in St. Lucia, with a similar layout for ease of transportation and movement—but all compacted into one giant building. The walkways were wide enough to allow golf carts and forklifts to drive to any section of this massive structure, which had several huge garage doors to allow them in and out. This made it easy to move produce out and inputs in.

In the greenhouse was a well-furnished office, a few enormous water tanks, carefully laid out hot water and irrigation lines, and lights throughout. The greenhouse was so large that each of the four sections had its own washrooms that were routinely cleaned every day. It also had a very large packhouse (for packaging produce) attached to it.

I lived very close to my workplace, with the bunkhouse less than fifty metres from the greenhouse entrance. It was a very strange feeling on my first morning to walk in snow to get to work. In the greenhouse, I had to walk a few hundred metres to get to my work area. In fact, the greenhouse was so large that when it came time for my twice-per-day fifteen-minute break, it took me five minutes just to get out of the greenhouse and run to the bunkhouse, even though the two buildings were right next to each other. I then had just five minutes to very quickly eat some food in order to have five minutes left to run back to my workstation before my break was up. This was especially frustrating because my workstation was on one end of the greenhouse, right next to the bunkhouse, but the greenhouse exit was in the middle of the building. So even though while I was working I could see the bicycles leaning up against the back wall of the bunkhouse, I had to run upwards of five hundred metres in the opposite direction just to get out the door. Those workers whose workstations were farther than mine would choose to spend their break in the greenhouse and forgo going to the bunkhouse where they could munch on something.

This was all a first for me. It felt like that one greenhouse could supply everyone in my home country with enough tomatoes and still have surplus to export. The structure left me wondering about all the careful thought that went into the planning and design and the huge initial cost that is associated with such an extensive fifty-plus-acre structure.

People tend to think that working on a farm means working for a small operation, owned and operated by a single farmer or a family. This could not have been further from the truth in my experience—and in the experience of many other migrant farm workers. The company I worked for is one of the biggest and most successful horticultural companies in Canada. It owns greenhouses and distribution centres across North America, employs well over a thousand people, and distributes produce from many other greenhouses and farms. Even though it's owned by a family, this is not a "family farm" in the way we normally think of it. This is a big business.

<><><>

Leamington is the tomato and greenhouse capital of Canada. It is also the migrant farm worker capital of Canada: each season it serves as the temporary home of thousands of migrant farm workers from the Caribbean, Mexico, Guatemala, Thailand, and other places in the Global South. Leamington specifically is known for its greenhouses, but the region surrounding it contains a wide array of farming operations— from labour-intensive fruit and vegetable farms to machine-harvested corn, wheat, and soy. The farms growing labour-intensive field crops also hire temporary foreign workers.

The farm where I worked grew tomatoes in greenhouses. Later on, they diversified and began to grow organic sweet peppers as well. As migrant workers, we know very little about the marketing or where the produce we grow is sold. But later I would come to learn that the tomatoes and sweet peppers from that greenhouse are distributed throughout Canada and the United States and can be found in the produce sections of many major supermarket chains.

I only found out that I would be going to Leamington a few days before I left St. Lucia. But that wasn't very important to me. I was provided with a document by the government officer who was serving me which had the name of the farm and some contact numbers. The officer said that it was a "good farm." Another migrant farm worker, who was at the office at that same time, also repeated that same power line: "That's a good farm." That was very comforting to hear. It was also comforting to hear that there were other St. Lucians working there. But at first, I didn't pay very close attention to this information. I was preoccupied with thoughts of working outside of my country for the first time and that I would be leaving my eleven- and thirteen-year-old children and my friends for eight months.

My contract began January 17 and expired in September of that year, for a total of eight months, the maximum allowed in the SAWP. On my first day on the farm, I remember the sixteen of us new migrant workers were all lined up and given a short orientation by our supervisor, covering the basic things we should know about our workplace and its operation. Orientation ended when we were asked to break up into two groups. Each group would work in a different section of the farm: one group went to the section of the greenhouse growing large tomatoes, while my group stayed in the section growing mini-tomatoes and experimental varieties. I heard that there were over three hundred different varieties in trial at that point in time. Thankfully, the temperature in the greenhouse stayed warm all winter, so I did not have to work in the cold.

Work in the greenhouse consisted of many different tasks. We carried out all the agronomic practices associated with the growing and production of tomatoes. By the time we arrived in January, the planting was already completed. Harvest didn't start until late February, but there was plenty of work to do until then, including removing leaves from plants (deleafing), and winding each tomato stem around a twine to make them grow vertically.

With my background in agriculture, I was very interested to learn about methods for growing crops in greenhouses. Of course, I had to pursue this learning entirely on my own, through observation and learning by doing. As a migrant farm worker, my level of education did not matter at work. There was no thought given to training foreign workers to understand the techniques being used or the science behind them. These are dead-end jobs—there is no room for advancement. For us migrant workers, it was obvious that we were only wanted in Canada for our hands, not our heads.

The first thing I noticed was that the tomatoes were not on the ground. They were being grown by the technique called hydroponics, a technique that is not very commonly used in St. Lucia. With hydroponics, the crop is not grown directly in the soil but in a different medium, with very frequent watering. At the greenhouse in Leamington, coconut fibres were used as the medium. I was surprised to see by-products of coconut, an important food crop in St. Lucia, being used in Canada as a soil substitute in agriculture. I noticed that each plant had two stems that kept growing and producing for the whole growing season, a phenomenon that I was witnessing for the first time. I was also surprised to see that the irrigation and fertilizing systems were automated—and that they used bees for pollination inside the greenhouse.

Harvest in the greenhouse usually starts in late February or early March. This activity was carried out two or three times per week until the end of the season, sometime in late October to November. Coming from St. Lucia, where I had not witnessed mega-greenhouse operations, that really stood out to me. On standard, outdoor farms—or even in smaller greenhouses like the one I'd operated back home—the harvesting period for most crops is, of course, quite short, meaning that farmers are at the mercy of whatever marketing conditions exist at harvest time, whether it's a glut or shortage in produce. But in the greenhouses in Canada, it was basically a continuous harvest, meaning that farmers had much less risk and a much more secure income.

I worked in two sections of the greenhouse: mini-tomatoes and assorted varieties. Each section was over five acres, consisting of

232 rows, with 500 stems (250 plants) in each row. Down the middle of each row ran two solid, two-inch metal pipes, a few inches off the ground and laid out just like train tracks. These pipes were multipurpose. They allowed the continuous flow of hot water that provided much-needed warmth to the plants and the greenhouse. They also served as tracks for the different carts workers used to perform their duties. This was the very definition of intensive agriculture.

The main jobs assigned to me and my co-workers were deleafing and picking (harvesting). Deleafing, just like the name suggests, means removing leaves from plants—specifically, bottom leaves. This was done in order to expose another layer of fruits, hastening ripening and making harvesting easier. It was a continuous task, performed throughout the long harvest season.

Both deleafing and harvesting entailed making your way, plant by plant, through those enormous rows of tomato plants. I can recall standing at the start of a row in my early days on the job, wondering how on earth I would be able to complete it at a fast pace. For deleafing, we worked on foot, sidestepping down the row while facing the plants, stopping briefly at each plant to quickly pick off a few bottom leaves before shifting down to the next one.

Harvesting was also a manual task, but it made use of those pipes that extended down each row. Pickers had carts that ran on the pipes, making it easy to push them forward. We would start the day with twenty empty plastic crates stacked on the cart, filling them with tomatoes as we went. Sometimes harvesting was more efficient when seated on the cart. Other times, depending on the variety and method of picking, standing was more efficient.

Once all twenty crates were full, the cart would be collected by a worker driving a small vehicle called a "tugger" that pulled upwards of a dozen carts, linked together like train cars. The tugger driver hauled the carts first to the scale to be weighed and then to the packhouse.

The fruits, which grow in clusters, were mostly picked as singles, most of the time with the fruit-stalk attached. Some varieties were harvested without the stalk attached. And some fruits were harvested in clusters of four, six, eight, and twelve fruits, using garden shears.

There were lots of different varieties of tomatoes. They were different in so many ways: fruit size, shape, and colour, for example. While the scientists conducting trials were interested in many qualities of the fruit, for us migrant workers, the most important things were how easy it was to pick and deleaf each variety. Some varieties were extremely easy to deleaf and harvest. Others were not so easy. The fact that a piece rate system was being used made those plant varieties our enemies. We knew the rows we should try to avoid, whenever possible.

Weeding was another job. Every other Saturday, I would go around the inner edges of the greenhouse perimeter to pull out weeds. This task starts in spring and runs throughout, until the end of the growing season. With monoculture it's easy for pests and disease to spread, even indoors, making weed control a critical activity.

Cleaning was another important task that I performed. The 232 rows in each section of the greenhouse where I worked were divided into two equal sections by an eight-foot-wide concrete centre aisle that was always littered with leaves and crushed tomatoes at the end of each workday. Those aisles were cleaned at the end of each day using a leaf blower—again, this was about preventing the spread of pests and disease that monoculture is very sensitive to.

A final task that I performed, especially in summertime peak season, was the packaging of tomatoes. That meant working some extra hours after my normal day's work.

◇◇◇

Not only was I adjusting to an unfamiliar crop and methods of production, but I also had to adapt to a completely new—and much more intense—way of working.

During the summer, we worked over sixty-six hours a week. Sometimes we worked fourteen hours or more in a day. In my first year, we worked Sunday to Sunday. All of this was without any overtime pay, as is standard under Ontario agricultural employment law. In fact, as I came to learn, many rules that offer protections to other workers do not apply in agriculture. Farm workers—whether they are migrants or Canadians—do not have mandated breaks, maximum hours of work, or guaranteed rest periods in between shifts.

In fact, it is worth quoting from the Government of Ontario's website, where it explains the "special rules or exemptions" for fruit, vegetable, and tobacco harvesters. The website informs workers of the following.

You are not entitled to:

- daily and weekly limits on hours of work
- daily rest periods
- time off between shifts
- weekly/bi-weekly rest periods
- eating periods
- overtime pay

The website goes on to tell workers: "You are entitled to public holidays and public holiday pay after you have worked for the same employer for at least 13 consecutive weeks."[31] Of course, for many migrant workers, their entire contract lasts less than thirteen weeks. Even for workers on eight-month contracts, like I was, that denies us public holidays for almost 40 percent of the duration of our employment each year. And in practice, most migrant workers don't even receive public holiday pay even after reaching thirteen weeks of employment.

These working conditions came as a total shock to me. It was so different to what I was accustomed to back home, where breaks for meals and rest are standard and where it is very unusual to work such long hours. And when you do work longer than eight hours, some overtime pay is granted.

We didn't just work long hours; we also worked at a breakneck pace. Greenhouse management made sure of that.

Every task that we performed was clocked. Each worker was given their own magnetic swipe card attached to a wristband, that we wore around our wrists like a watch. Each worker's card had their employee number printed on it. At the beginning of each day, we clocked in, and if you were one minute late, you would be deducted fifteen minutes' pay, with escalating penalties from there. Of course, we were always eager to please our employer and arrived ahead of time, so we never found out exactly what those penalties were.

From the moment we clocked in, our productivity was being constantly monitored. There were stations scattered at intervals throughout the greenhouse at the front of rows, which were on the side of the wide centre aisles. For every activity you performed, you had to swipe your card after completing it, along with the code for the activity (harvesting, deleafing, winding and clipping, and so on). The system would track what activity was performed, where it was performed, your output, and how fast you worked. At any time, the supervisor could check which rows you had worked and how much time you were taking. The clocking system had a dual purpose: it was a powerful tool for surveillance, and it also kept us running all day long.

It felt like we were being pushed. We would push ourselves above and beyond to meet, and even exceed, our employer's expectations. We would skip our washroom breaks just to maintain our work speed. Energy drinks, something I never used in my home country, were now a normal part of my diet. During my first few years, my roommate and good buddy, Anthony Charles, a.k.a. "Blackie" (who is convinced that we are related), would start work half an hour before the scheduled start time. We would cut our lunch hour short by over twenty minutes just to meet our employer's expectations.

A lot of the pressure came from the structure of the program. As migrant workers, we are "permanently temporary." In order to be sure of keeping our spot in the program, we need to be requested by our employer to return each year. Additionally, the threat of deportation hangs over our heads at all times. Employers in the program can send workers home if they are not happy with them, with basically no oversight. Making matters worse, migrant workers do not have a good understanding of what our rights are; we are isolated in rural communities, invisible, with neither support nor recourse.

At the end of each week, management would put a listing on the board displaying workers' names in three colour codes indicating the speed we were performing at. The people who did really well would be on top, their names displayed with a green background. And those who did really poorly would be at the bottom, in red. This tool created conflicts and worked well for our employer: a population fighting itself cannot fight back.

The supervisor—I'll call him Carlos—would scold people who found themselves consistently at the bottom, telling them, "Look here, you see that there are guys at the top? That means that the work can be done. I want you to be there at the top of the list. And remember in St. Lucia there's a hundred guys who are willing to take your spot." (I overheard this sort of warning made to St. Lucian co-workers on at least two occasions.)

We interpreted this statement as a threat that workers who did not meet a certain standard would not be requested to return to the farm the following year—or worse, that they might be sent home early. Threats like Carlos's are extremely common on farms that employ migrant workers.

Of course, this was quite disturbing to the men hearing it. In St. Lucia, we're not accustomed to this sort of thing. Workplace culture is typically much less authoritarian, and of course, our employers do not have the power to deport us.

A story from my second year in the program shows the type of situation that migrant workers can easily face. That year, one of my co-workers was fired and booked on a flight to be repatriated to St. Lucia. The supposed reason was his slow speed of work. I say "supposed" because the piece rate chart showed that some workers were slower than him. Before being fired, he was given a verbal warning and showed some slight improvement after that. But it was not enough. Within a few days he was told he was fired and would be sent home.

The worker tried to plead his case, explaining that he needed a bit more time to tie up some loose ends—to save some more money and complete his purchases of goods to ship home. Management paid no regard to this. Less than a week after his first warning, he was booked on a return flight to St. Lucia. He never actually boarded that flight, however. Instead, he decided to leave the farm and stay in Canada without legal immigration status. With no opportunity to remain in Canada legally, this is a difficult decision that migrant workers occasionally make.

Being fired during the season wasn't the only way to be let go. Each year, some workers were not asked back to the farm. Sometimes, that would mean that they were out of the SAWP altogether. This happened to my co-worker and close friend Blackie. About midway through my time on the program, Blackie was not requested to return to the farm. As is typical in these cases, he received no explanation for why he was let go. He believes it had to do with the no-nonsense senior manager—Blackie heard through the grapevine that the manager did not like his style of walking, calling it "lazy." Like so much in the SAWP, workers are left in the dark on these matters and forced to guess the reasons for their fate.

Carlos, the supervisor who reminded us of how easily we could be replaced, was Latin American but had lived in Canada for a long time. He was bilingual in English and Spanish. When I think of Carlos, I am reminded of an advertisement about a painkiller: It's tough on pain but gentle on you. Carlos was always approachable, but he was tough when it came to getting us to produce.

Carlos was on the front line and in direct contact with us every-day. He moved about in the greenhouse by bicycle. That way, he was within reach of everyone. Carlos paid attention to each worker and listened very well. He tried to match each worker to a job that they were good at. Carlos tried to befriend us and helped us in many ways—for example, bringing us pharmacy items (like creams for muscle pain relief) or ordering things for us online. He even made an effort to learn some St. Lucian Creole. He did not want us to see him as a man who was always carrying a big stick.

Carlos was the one who drove us to town every Friday evening, for our weekly shopping trips, when we bought groceries, sent money home via Western Union, and ran other errands. On those days, the last bus back to the farm would arrive around 10 p.m. Carlos's workday would end then.

Carlos was our direct supervisor, but in such a big operation there was, of course, a large management structure above him. Each of the four sections of the greenhouse had a grower (responsible for growing healthy plants) and a supervisor. Above them was the no-nonsense senior manager, who I think was appointed by the owner (who I never, ever saw). That senior manager never, ever smiled when he was around. All the supervisors and growers would accompany him when he made his routine rounds in the greenhouse. We always had an idea when he would be making these rounds, because everything had to be perfect. No one ever wanted to disappoint him.

The no-nonsense attitude of the senior manager was represent-ative of our overall treatment in the program. There is an immense power imbalance between migrant workers and our employers (and their appointed managers and supervisors). Sometimes that power went to their heads. I can recall a few occasions when supervisors made some inappropriate—and even cruel—comments to migrant workers. "If you only knew how much money I'm making off you" was one such comment. Even worse was "We own you all." As for us migrant workers, with the pressure we feel to provide for our families and the threat of deportation always looming over our heads, we are scared into working and living under difficult conditions and accepting such verbal abuse.

The element of fear is built into the SAWP and serves as a powerful tool for employers. A populace in fear cannot fight back.

Chapter 12
MORE ON WORKING IN THE GREENHOUSE

In St. Lucia, it is a common practice to have fixed piece rates, where your work output is fixed or set for the week. In Canada, for the first time, I was introduced to what I call a variable piece rate system. The latter is a modern whip that's used to keep workers running throughout the day.

In the greenhouse in Leamington, the output and pace of work always changes. It's like trying to score a goal and they keep on shifting the goalposts—you never know where they are. It is like being in a dark room, where you can never tell whether you will be sitting on a soft chair or on a chair of thorns.

For example, if one week I harvested 2,000 pounds of tomatoes, my name could be in green, at the top of the list. The next week I might harvest 2,200 pounds, but I wouldn't be in the green, because another person harvested 2,500 pounds or more. In that way, the expected output and pace of work kept on changing.

The piece rate system was only explained verbally. There was nothing in writing. Very few of us understood it. Management manipulated this system to their advantage. The workers claimed that only one or very few people at the very top of the list benefited financially. In any event, the amount of the supposed bonus was never disclosed.

I can clearly remember the times when I found myself at the bottom of the list. At the start of the growing season, before picking was in full swing and when some workers were still in St. Lucia, I was assigned the task of winding plants. The growing tip of the plant is very delicate. Not wanting to damage the plants, I took extra care in handling them, meaning that it took me a very long time to perform that task. I found myself consistently at the bottom of the list during that period, which lasted a month or so. This bothered me because I was always trying to improve, but it just wasn't working for me with this task.

After a couple weeks of doing it, my name was still at the bottom of the list. Not wanting to disappoint my employers, I took the initiative to speak to Carlos about my struggles. His response was surprising and a great relief. He said he was happy with my work since there was very little breakage. He said to bear with him and keep doing my best until the other batch of workers arrived, since they would be taking over that task. Every week, the faster guys would come over to help me after they completed their allotted quota of rows.

We constantly felt pressured to go as fast as possible, to go above and beyond. Workers would use things like energy drinks, especially during the afternoon break, to keep them going through the long afternoons on harvesting days. Many felt that they had to go a hundred miles an hour from start to finish. Others would say the race is not for the speediest, but for those who can endure.

Since almost everything was paid by piece rate—per pound for harvesting and per plant for winding and deleafing—the faster you worked, the more you were supposed to earn. But even during the many times when I was in the green as a picker, I did not notice any increase in my pay beyond the minimum wage. At the end of the day, it was the company that profited from the variable piece rate system.

Many factors come into play with how fast you are able to work. Different varieties of tomatoes, for example, take more or less time to harvest. In general, the smaller the tomato, the more difficult it is—and therefore the longer it takes—to harvest.

In the greenhouse where I worked, there were several varieties of tomatoes. As pickers, we were interested in how big and heavy they were and how easy they were to pick. Pickers harvesting in rows with small tomatoes were placed in competition with pickers harvesting bigger, heavier fruits. Our work was evaluated by the total weight picked. With a variable piece rate system, no consideration is given to whether a worker is very experienced at a particular task or if they are just learning it. Though the playing field wasn't level for all workers, we were all measured by the same yardstick. Output was the only thing being measured and nothing else.

On the farm where I lived and worked, there were two Barbadians, about sixty St. Lucians, sixty Guatemalans, and thirty Jamaicans—all men and ranging in age from early twenties to sixties. We St. Lucians always wanted to prove to management that we were better workers than the Barbadians. Similarly, the Barbadians wanted to outperform the Jamaicans, and the Jamaicans wanted to outperform the Guatemalans. It was just instilled in us that we wanted to outdo each other. And with management's weekly ranking of workers' output, we were directly pitted against each other and among ourselves. Language and culture also kept us separated. The piece rate system exploited that weakness among us.

The migrant workers on the farm were all men, and the overall workforce on the farm (including Canadian and immigrant workers) was mostly male. There were some women employed in the packhouse (boxing tomatoes). Occasionally the farm hired local temporary workers at peak times, and there were sometimes women in these crews. But by and large, the farm was an overwhelmingly male environment.

When I was on the farm, I heard that, many years earlier, there were far more Barbadians on the farm than St. Lucians. But over time the St. Lucians were able to elbow out the Barbadians, supposedly because St. Lucians complained much less and had a superior work ethic. By the time I got there, there were only two Barbadians.

I also heard that before I worked there, there were no Guatemalans. The only Spanish workers there were from Mexico. I heard through the grapevine that the Mexicans had begun to band together to fight back against their poor working conditions. This was something the employer could not tolerate. The Canadian food system is designed to make it easy for employers to go to another country and get workers to replace perceived troublemakers. So I understood the Guatemalans were brought in to replace the Mexicans after they acted collectively to resist the system that they found was unfair.

We witnessed high turnover among the few Canadians who came to work in the greenhouse. Some would start in the morning and quit by lunchtime. Occasionally students came to work for short periods of time. It was rare to see a student last for more than four to six weeks or so.

Canadian workers worked at their own pace—something that was obvious to us migrant workers. They also did not receive the same pressure from supervisors about their work or pace. Their names were not listed on the board where migrant workers' productivity was displayed, so they were not pushed in the same way as we were. The key difference, of course, is that they were not on a tied work permit, with the threat of deportation hanging over them. They could afford to take their time, even if it meant being fired. We migrant workers did not have that luxury.

Our very different pace of work meant that we didn't interact much with Canadian workers in the greenhouse—we were always going faster, so we would quickly leave them behind. There was one occasion when I was able to compare my work output with a Canadian's. One morning, the packhouse workers—mostly local Canadians and permanent immigrants, with a small subsection of migrant workers—were called to help out with the picking, in order to have enough tomatoes to start packing operations after the ten o'clock morning break. When breaktime came, I was able to see the progress of one Canadian packhouse worker. She was on her third crate, I was on my eighteenth.

I have often heard that it takes five or more Canadians to do the work of one migrant farm worker. That may not be a precise statistic, but my experience in the greenhouse definitely showed migrant workers to be head and shoulders above Canadian workers in terms of productivity.

For most of my first year on the farm, I worked Sunday to Sunday. No rest days. During my second year, in 2013, a Sunday rest day was introduced. I heard through the grapevine that some of the tomato buyers had expressed concern about how the workers were being treated and that this was the reason a rest day was introduced. But I don't know for sure. It was not something that came from the workers. We felt that we could never question things. We knew that if we spoke up, it would be a problem. And that we were expected to be ambassadors for our countries.

◇◇◇

Generally, we worked from sunrise to sunset. During the short winter days in January, before harvesting began, we worked from about 7 a.m. to 5 p.m. But as the hours of daylight got longer, so, too, did the hours we worked. My first summer in Canada was a shocker. It was very strange for me to experience sunset between 9:30 and 10 p.m.

Temperature and day length is very predictable and stable in St. Lucia, a tropical country. Being in a temperate country for the first time was a major experience for me.

The moment harvesting started, everything changed. In the summer, we worked long hours. Especially when I was doing packaging. We still started at 7 a.m., but packaging could run as late as nine, ten, or eleven o'clock at night. Some guys would finish way later than that depending on the task or the order they were working on. And then we would be back to work again the next morning at seven. So in the summertime it was always long hours of work—and often in extreme heat. The summer heat inside of a greenhouse—which was more intense than outdoors—was a living hell for us. We would perspire at such a fast rate that our clothing would get completely wet. It was like being out in the rain without an umbrella or raincoat.

Most of the time, our schedules were pretty stable and predictable. But often enough, especially during the summer, we had no idea what our day at work would be like. At very short notice, we would be "asked" to work overtime, which often meant being assigned to another task. I put asked in quotation marks because we felt like we had no other choice. That was the time when we worked twelve or more hours in a day and an average of sixty-six per week—without, as I've already mentioned, overtime pay. A few workers were asked to work even more hours than the rest of us. They eagerly agreed, since workers typically wanted to work as many hours as possible in order to earn more money.

Of course, there was a downside to working more hours, and these privileged few struggled with getting sufficient rest and eating proper meals. This was also a technique used to pit workers against each other. Workers not getting those hours would be envious, while those getting the extra time would do what it took to protect their higher status. It was said that these workers were the eyes and the ears of management in the bunkhouse.

Even into the fall, we would continue to work long hours when more production was needed or when cleaning was in full speed in preparation for the next growing season. They would bring in lights to allow us to work past sunset in November and December. With such long work hours, we often didn't get enough sleep. Sometimes workers were so tired that they would start to nod off during the workday if they were performing a task with some waiting time, such as applying pesticides.

We were never in contact with the ground or any mud in the greenhouse because the entire floor was covered with plastic. The upper side was white and the side facing the ground was black. The plastic solved one problem but created another by allowing water from busted irrigation lines to accumulate and form a pool that wet our feet, shoes, and socks. With time, these pools of stagnant water would grow moss that released unpleasant smells into the air.

Working long, intense hours was difficult enough, but unsafe working conditions were even more concerning. Sometime during the summer of my first year, some co-workers noticed that pesticides were being sprayed only a few rows away from where we were working. At that time I was so focused on my living conditions that this didn't alarm me as much as it should have. Fortunately, my co-workers recognized the danger and immediately reported it to Carlos. In another example of how Carlos looked out for our best interests, he took the issue seriously and made changes that ensured that it wouldn't happen again—banning spraying in areas where workers were present and arranging for more spraying to occur during the night.

To many Canadians, these might seem like obvious policies that should have been in place all along. But the reality of migrant farm labour in Canada is that many workers have to work under unsafe conditions, with no sympathy or concern from their employers or supervisors. As an activist, I still occasionally hear similar stories of pesticides being sprayed close to workers in the greenhouse or field.

It is never as straightforward or easy as it should be for workers to simply report the issue and get it corrected. With all the pressures to work hard and cause as little trouble as possible, migrant workers feel a disincentive to report unsafe working conditions. So many workers have been fired and blacklisted from the program for "complaining" too much.[32] These workers have basically no recourse. With families back home relying on the income, most of us don't want to become another one of these horror stories. So it is often easier to just stay quiet—especially on farms without a sympathetic middleman like Carlos, as we were fortunate to have.

There were lots of things that could cause injury in the greenhouse. It was not uncommon for workers to slip or trip on the plastic greenhouse floors, which could be wet or uneven. I knew a few workers who twisted their ankles in this way. Another cause of injury were the scissor carts that carried workers up and down the rows as they wound and clipped the tomato plants. Even if you aren't familiar with the term "scissor carts," you've probably seen them (or something similar) before. They are small vehicles with a platform that can rise up, allowing workers to reach high places. When they are extended, you can see the criss-crossing, hinged steel beams that support the platform; when lowered all the way, the beams fold down until they lie flat—similar to the blades of scissors coming together.

Anyway, when the scissor carts were extended to the growing tips of the plants—ten feet high or more—and travelled over uneven rails, it could cause the cart to topple, unexpectedly throwing the worker riding in the cart off balance. Workers using the cart were not provided with harnesses, so in these situations it was easy to be thrown out of the cart and fall to the ground. This exact scenario happened to a Jamaican colleague and friend at the greenhouse. He was thrown out of a toppled scissor cart and suffered a broken pelvic bone.

I had a few close calls myself while working in the greenhouse. On Saturdays when I worked on the inner edges of the perimeter of the greenhouse pulling out weeds, I had to climb the metal bars that held each row up. Those bars had sharp edges. Sometimes my shoes got wet from water on the ground and became slippery when climbing on those metal bars. Every year, between the scissor carts, ground conditions, and risky tasks, there were multiple reports of workers suffering injuries of varying degrees.

The farm had a joint health and safety committee that had a worker representative. I have no idea how that worker ever got selected for such an important position. However, though injuries remained common, they did consult with me on matters of workplace health and safety on a couple of occasions.

◇◇◇

While there was a lot that was concerning in greenhouse work, it wasn't all bad. What really made greenhouse work tolerable—and sometimes even enjoyable—were the people. We passed the time by getting to know each other, making jokes, and teasing each other. Though in the bunkhouse I lived with my fellow St. Lucians, in the greenhouse I had a chance to get to know the Guatemalans and Jamaicans on the farm. Although language was a clear barrier with the Guatemalans and the piece rate made us competitors, the constant search for humour united us.

I had a lot of fun with one Guatemalan worker, let's call him José. José often picked on another worker, whom I'll call Nicodemo. Nicodemo was a little person who was very competitive and super sensitive. Sometimes José called Nicodemo "astronauta calor" (hot astronaut), a name he got because he had to dress in a white disposable suit, like an astronaut, every time he had to wind and clip in rows with diseased plants. That disposable coverall kept Nicodemo very hot on the scissor lift, twelve feet or so up in the air, working in the direct sunlight that shone through the plastic covering of the greenhouse. He was so competitive that every second mattered to him; he always wanted to place first on the piece rate chart. So the fact that he had to take the time to dress in and out of the astronaut suit multiple times per day annoyed Nicodemo greatly. Nicodemo's obsession with going for the hundred-dollar incentive that supposedly went to the top worker earned him a variation on the nickname from José: "astronauta cien" ("astronaut one hundred"). Nicodemo disliked both nicknames just as much as he disliked José, who he called "no good." Their constant bickering made me chuckle.

One Saturday, very close to the end of the workday, many of us were working in the final row of the day. When we shared work in the same row, each person had to clock the percentage of the row that they had completed. For that row, we were each clocking roughly 15 percent. Then in the dying moments before the final bell, a friendly young Vietnamese lady came to join us in the last row. Though she had only helped for about five minutes, José insisted that she should clock in 50 percent of the row. From that day on, we've been calling José "50 percent" and laughing about it.

"Big Bird," a Jamaican, was another regular source of entertainment in the greenhouse. He was tall, big, and loud—but friendly. He would tell the Guatemalans, especially Nicodemo and José, in loud Jamaican patois, that they have no respect. Everyone would just laugh. Because of his build, no one wanted to challenge him.

I enjoyed interacting with the other Guatemalan workers as well. Some Guatemalans played Spanish music all the time, and it was especially loud on harvesting days. Bachata Romántica was their favourite genre. Though I could not understand the lyrics, I found the music very enjoyable. They were always happy to translate the lyrics or simply tell me what it was all about. Every time our paths crossed in the greenhouse, I would shout out "Bachata Romántica!" That would bring out a smile and a laugh. With time they began to refer to me as "Manticaro," a playful rearrangement of the word "Romántica," and they still call me that to this day.

◇◇◇

During my first season in Canada, I felt like I was playing a game that I loved, but whose rules I didn't know. What do I mean by that? I love agriculture. Being raised in the countryside, agriculture has been my passion for much of my life. And I was looking forward to working in agriculture in Canada and learning more about it.

I took comfort in knowing that the SAWP was a legal program with the blessing of both my government and the Canadian government—and that I would be supported by a representative of the St. Lucian government. How can things go wrong if the government was on my side? That was my reasoning.

But reality revealed otherwise. I felt like nothing had prepared me for the roller-coaster ride of being a migrant farm worker in Canada.

I came to realize that my strong point drove me to my weak point. My strong point was agriculture, my passion. But pursuing that passion in Canada drove me to my weak point, to those poor living and working conditions that I did not expect and did not enjoy. The thing I love took me to the conditions I least expected.

There was a big gap between my expectations of Canada and the reality. I, like most Canadians, assumed everything was all right and there would be no cause for complaint or reason for alarm. The sad truth is that in Canada, it is legal to exploit the soil, the environment, and migrant farm workers. This was a profoundly disappointing discovery for me.

Perhaps my biggest challenge being in Canada was coming to terms with all of this. I call it calming my mind: to bridge that gap between my expectation and reality, to understand things, and to accept my new reality. But that was just a short-term survival strategy. In the longer term, I had no interest in accepting the conditions of migrant workers, and instead would direct my understanding towards transforming Canada's exploitative farm labour system.

Chapter 13
BUNKHOUSE LIFE

I lived on the farm where I worked.

After our long, hard days working in the greenhouse, we came back to the bunkhouse, our accommodations for the season. Our bunkhouse was called the "Caribbean bunkhouse" (since it housed West Indian workers) or the "new bunkhouse" (since it was the newer of the two on the farm). The new bunkhouse was a large, single-storey, concrete building, about 100 feet by 50 feet.

The front yard and entrance to the bunkhouse was the only noticeable area of the farm that was unpaved. While the rest of the farm was kept looking neat and clean, the yard outside the bunkhouse was often muddy, with pools of water stagnating long after rainfalls.

The bunkhouse was shared between sixty-two workers, with a wide age range: from early twenties to sixties. We had sixty St. Lucians and two very friendly Barbadians who were around sixty years old and had worked in the SAWP for over twenty years. The St. Lucians came from all parts of the island—mainly from rural zones, not surprisingly—with the quarters (equivalent to provinces) of Dennery and Castries (the rural section, not the city) especially well represented. The majority had been on the program for many seasons, but there were also newcomers like me and the fifteen others who had travelled with me from St. Lucia.

Seven rooms housed eight workers each, and one room accommodated six. The standard rooms were about twenty by fifteen feet, with eight workers divided between four bunk beds with upper and lower berths. Each room had a small window and two vents. These vents supplied much-needed warm air during winter and cool air in the summer. Coming from St. Lucia, this type of heating and cooling system was completely new to me and the other new arrivals. On many occasions, roommates of mine would complain about the smell of food coming to the room early in the morning through the vent.

The lower berths are always in high demand by the workers. Very few people like the upper bunk because it is a little challenging to climb up and down. Luckily for me, an acquaintance from back home, Thomas (nicknamed "Colochito" or "Alie"), had arrived to the farm before me and cleverly saved a lower berth for me. That was very significant for me. I'm somebody—especially in the cold—who frequents the washroom. You can imagine the amount of damage I would do to my bladder being in the upper bunk and not wanting to wake up my roommates by going up and down. So he helped me in that sense. I'm extremely grateful for that.

Some workers went to great lengths to decorate their lower bunks. Not only did they enclose them with cardboard and bed sheets, but they also had their entertainment carefully fitted in there, installing portable televisions and DVD players, small fans, and lights, among other things.

With four bunk beds and a small plastic table with four chairs in the middle, the room was crowded. There was very little space to put our suitcases, clothing, and other personal belongings. It was really tight. And what made it even worse was that during the eight-month period, we tried to accumulate goods to take back home—a variety of carpentry, masonry, landscaping, and auto mechanic tools, small appliances like microwaves, clothing, shoes, electronics, non-perishable food items, and more. That would take up space too, so over the season the room became even more crowded. Workers sometimes also purchased large appliances like washers and refrigerators to take back home, but fortunately these were usually stored in the common area of the bunkhouse where there was a bit more space.

Sleeping in a room with seven other men, the most common enemy and complaint of all workers was snoring. Although few workers were guilty of such behaviour, they were never forgiven for it. At nightfall and bedtime, they became enemy number one.

We had a wall-mounted rack somewhere near each bunk bed to hang our clothes (shared between the two men in each bunk), but no closets or dressers. There were very small lockers where we could store our everyday goods, like powdered milk and sugar. But there weren't enough lockers for everyone—there were maybe six per room. The lighting in the room was the same kind of fluorescent bulbs that were used in the greenhouse, so you could see that it wasn't a home. This was pointed out to me by an artist friend who came to visit our farm.

Each room was equipped with a washroom. Of course, everybody would need it more or less at the same time, especially in the morning to get ready for work.

In one sense we were very lucky with our room. At one point during the season, some of the other rooms had problems with bedbugs, and I heard that in the past the entire bunkhouse had been infested.

We did our own cooking. For sixty-two workers, there were just three stoves; one had eight burners, so there were a total of sixteen. Everyone in the bunkhouse shared a walk-in refrigerator, approximately eight by eight feet. There were about five microwaves, and maybe four or five freezers (a couple of chest freezers and couple upright), so more than ten workers had to share a freezer. Freezers were especially important for storing meat—with the constant traffic in and out of the walk-in refrigerator, it was not a good idea to keep meat in there.

With such a large bunkhouse, we never knew exactly who we were sharing the freezer with. We would mark our goods, but sometimes things would disappear, and you would never know if something had gone missing or if somebody had moved it to another freezer. A common phrase in the bunkhouse was, There's a rat in the freezer! Refrigerator and freezer space was an issue especially after shopping day on Fridays. Wherever the space was, you used it. It was a free-for-all.

Just like with the bathrooms, demand for the kitchen appliances came at the same time each day, with everyone rushing to get their meals. In our culture we try to cook something fresh from scratch every day, but because of work pressure, most of my colleagues would cook food to last more than one day. That made the use of microwaves extremely important, especially at lunchtime, when everybody would rush to use them during the same lunch hour.

Next to the kitchen was the common area, with picnic tables and a television. This was the eating area, the living area, and the social area. There were no sofas or other comfortable seating. Just like the bedrooms, the common area was lit by ultra-bright, uninviting fluorescent bulbs. It was not a very relaxing atmosphere.

The limited access to bathroom, kitchen, and other facilities gave us lots of reasons to fight and compete with each other in the bunkhouse. What some of us found to be annoying was a source of entertainment for others. Access to burners, microwaves, and kitchen sinks were daily battles. In the evening the TV would take centre stage. There was one television for the whole bunkhouse. The two television programs that kept us united, and prevented us from fighting among ourselves, were, ironically, wrestling and cricket.

The weekend was the time to fight over the laundry: with just four washing machines and four dryers for sixty-two guys, access to washers and dryers was difficult throughout the weekend. It was not uncommon to see people going in and out of the laundry at odd hours of the night. Dryers were another thing that was completely new to me. In rural St. Lucia, we hang our laundry on clotheslines and let the sun do the work.

The house had just two telephone lines and no internet. Those telephones couldn't receive calls—you could only make calls from them, using a calling card. That is hard on workers and their faraway families, for families not to be able to call their loved ones. We asked management repeatedly to provide internet to the bunkhouse, but our attempts were in vain. By the time I left the farm after four years, there was still no internet. Not very many workers had cell phones. The plans were expensive and covered things such as Canada-wide calling and local texting that were not useful to guys who primarily wanted to contact family and friends back home.

Later on, when I became an activist with Justicia for Migrant Workers, I saw many migrant bunkhouses around Ontario and elsewhere, and I came to realize that the conditions at my farm, as disheartening as they were, were on the whole above average. Many migrant worker bunkhouses are makeshift buildings—remodelled barns or warehouses, for example. It is common in these types of bunkhouses to have one enormous room with dozens of bunkbeds jammed in, with nearly every square inch of space taken up by workers' modest belongings. They are often dimly lit, with few windows and poor air circulation. Some bunkhouses have no washrooms or kitchens—workers must go to a separate building for those needs. Some have poor water quality and workers are advised to boil water before drinking it. Bunkhouses often have insufficient appliances—ten or more workers to a fridge or stove, for example. It is also common for employers to forbid visitors to bunkhouses—or require workers to get permission before having visitors. I often see signs at bunkhouse entrances that say exactly that: "Private Property. No visitors without permission." As if migrant workers, in a foreign country, often in remote rural areas, did not feel isolated enough already, employer policies like these guarantee it.

It was emasculating as a grown man—with a family, a home, and life of my own—to give up my privacy and share a bedroom with seven other guys. I felt like my manhood—and my freedom—were being taken away. It was also heartbreaking to be away from my family. In your home country you go to work, but at the end of the day you report to your family. It was difficult to come to terms with being away from my family for eight months of the year. In St. Lucia, generally when you return home from work your meal will be ready or certain tasks will be done, but in Canada, you have to do everything: your meals, your dishes, your laundry. You have to do all of that. You have no privacy and you're not doing it on your own time. You have to compete with people—to get a spot at the stove or for the washing machine. It was extraordinarily difficult to come to terms with those living conditions.

Another thing I had to give up was my nickname, Ricky, that I had gone by my whole life. There were two of us with that same name in my bunkhouse room. To make communication easier, I agreed to give up my nickname and go by my Christian name, Gabriel, instead. I didn't realize how much trouble this would give me. People would call me Gabriel and I would ignore them or not respond, being completely unaccustomed to that name. Going by a new name all of a sudden reinforced my feelings of having lost some of my independence, my personhood.

◇◇◇

As difficult as bunkhouse life could be, friendships with co-workers made everything much easier to handle. The sixteen of us who had flown together from St. Lucia formed a group. We only met one another for the first time at our short orientation session and then at the airport in Castries. But we were all first-timers and all headed to the same farm. That united us, made it easy for us to gel a little.

The sixteen of us were split between two rooms in the bunkhouse, rooms 7 and 8 (directly opposite each other). While everybody else on the farm cooked their own individual meals, we as a group cooked together. They called us "One Love." We would cook our food together, shop together, do everything together. Most other workers found that very strange. But we tried to gel together and encourage and motivate each other and stay united. That was really helpful for me to get through the early days of my first season in Canada.

My roommates and I—eight of us, half of One Love—also organized a "susu" together. Now what is that? A susu is an informal group of people who come together and periodically contribute a portion of money, with lump-sum payouts rotating between the members. In our case, every Friday we would contribute $100 and we would rotate who got the $700 lump sum each week. Susu is a common practice in the West Indies, though it goes by different names. In Jamaica they call it "partner." I remember hearing that the tradition originally came from Africa, but I'm not too sure. I know people from the Caribbean who are living in Toronto and keeping the tradition alive.

The moment I stopped focusing on myself and started to look beyond my disappointing living conditions, I discovered how interesting life in the bunkhouse was. From that moment, my entertainment in the bunkhouse was endless and free. We had lots of interesting characters.

We had characters who were notorious for forgetting their pots on the stove until they began to smoke, causing the energy level of the entire bunkhouse to rise in excitement. We had a character who was extremely forgetful and would forget his belongings anywhere and everywhere. The chorus of teasing that sung out to him on Friday nights, after we returned from shopping, was a highlight of our payday. Another character was always last-minute in preparing for work. He was always running to make up for his lateness. His work speed, however, overshadowed his shortcomings.

One character who makes me laugh to this day was a very fair skinned roommate of mine that everyone in the bunkhouse called "Sheamus," named after a very popular redhead wrestler. At first, we called him "yellow," but once we saw the real Sheamus wrestling on TV, my roommate's name changed. The resemblance was uncanny. Moses (his real name) was a very jovial guy and accepted his nickname with good humour.

Two of my favourite characters in the bunkhouse were "Sheeny" and "Curry." Their funny-looking haircuts (shaved on the sides with a large Afro on top) were a source of entertainment for the rest of us. Just like Moses, Sheeny and Curry had good senses of humour and played along with the joke. I think they even enjoyed the attention that their haircuts attracted.

Some characters in the bunkhouse were very enterprising. There were barbers. There were DJs who recorded CDs and music on memory cards for other workers and even participated in DJ competitions at nightclubs. There were guys who sold phone cards. There were others who sold beer, other alcoholic drinks, and cigarettes. Then there was that ever-smiling Christian colleague who sold strictly non-alcoholic drinks, which were very popular during lunchtime. A few workers came with other skills such as auto repair and body work. They found time to generate additional income, using church and other networks to find odd jobs. Some other guys tried to make extra money by gambling, staying up very late to play cards, mostly during the weekends. Despite the fact that migrant farm workers are deemed "unskilled," seemingly everyone in the bunkhouse had a skill and a time when he was in high demand.

The bunkhouse entrepreneurs weren't the only people selling things in the bunkhouse. Even though we were isolated in rural Ontario, vendors came to the farm from Toronto and elsewhere, to sell all kinds of things: electronics, phones, phone cards, shoes, clothing, jewellery, a lot of dry goods. Occasionally people would come and sell fish, eggs, and other fresh items. Another vendor would sell prepared meals. These vendors specialized in selling to migrant farm workers. They would travel from farm to farm making their rounds. They were so regular that they offered credit and layaway terms.

Other workers had special skills and were frequently called upon to help out their colleagues. Some were experts in packing the barrels and crates that workers stuffed full of their accumulated goods to ship home. They made sure every inch of space was occupied—that was an art. My job in this process was to write the destination addresses on the barrels. The few colleagues with IT skills were constantly kept busy helping others with their phones and accessories. Fish cleaning was a skill very few had (or at least a task that very few liked). The few who did were in high demand in the bunkhouse. Everyone had a skill, and everyone had a time when he was in demand.

Some of the guys were very elaborate with their cooking, especially those who worked in the kitchens at tourist hotels in St Lucia. They occupied the entire kitchen for what seemed like eternity. The bakers added to the culture in the bunkhouse. The pleasant smell of fresh-baked bread was always a great delight. Homemade bread is our preference in St. Lucia.

Then there was the bunkhouse gossip, politics, and teasing. Certain guys would pick up on every minute detail about everyone else, collecting material that could be turned into gossip, a story, or a joke. Any little thing could put you on the receiving end—clothing, for example. Guys who always wore long pants and never shorts were picked on. And the guy who never removed his hat was quietly gossiped about.

There was fresh news every day. Saturday, the day after payday, was the most notorious, when we would hear about the financial and relationship issues of many of our colleagues. One of the bunkhouse's telephones was in the hallway close to my room. Often guys had to speak very loudly to make themselves heard over the noise. That took away their privacy and they fell prey to the hungry gossipers in the bunkhouse. The tale-tellers were referred to as "talking giants" and said to be even more talkative than some women, both common ways to describe gossipers in St. Lucia. The loudest and most respected "talking giant" was nicknamed "Sixteen." He had so much influence. He was like the mainstream media of the bunkhouse.

I found myself in the unenviable headlines of the gossip news going around one day, when I introduced a green light bulb to our room, without consulting or informing my roommates. I thought it was a noble idea to have a light that was not so bright in the room. To my complete surprise, the talk was that I was turning the bunkhouse into a dancehall with disco lights. As some guys would say, the tomato plants in the greenhouse have eyes and ears. Nothing would go unnoticed in the bunkhouse.

Bunkhouse politics operated in a delicate balance. Guys often had to be especially delicate with inviting visitors into the bunkhouse or into their rooms. For example, when churchgoers invited local members of the church to the bunkhouse, it could make non-Christian workers feel uncomfortable and like they had to behave in a certain way. And vice versa, when the non-Christian workers would invite people over for parties, with drinking and loud music and so on, it would make the Christian workers uncomfortable. Another example: when guys with family members in Toronto (about four hours' drive from Leamington) invited them to visit, it could spark envy in those without relatives in Ontario.

In some of the more challenging moments during my first year in the program, I was helped a lot by colleagues who were strong-willed and strong-minded. A few co-workers and friends in particular held my hand to go through that stage. Curry, the character with the wild haircut, was one of them. I cannot remember exactly their choice of words, but they were the ones who really helped to provide comfort during that time. Mentally, I wasn't ready for the poor living and working conditions that I found in Canada. That was the last thing I expected. I expected everything to be smooth and seamless, since I was not going through a private labour recruiter, but through the government. I assumed they would have my best interests at heart. But as the realities of the program were revealed, it was those stronger guys, who were not only talkative, but also inspiring, who helped pull me through and keep our group together.

In the early days there were two other people who were really helpful to me. The first person was my niece Camilla (also known as Gwen), who lives in Brampton. I would call her really often and she was always positive. The second was my aunt, Aunty Lena Hayes-Moise, in the United States, who has since passed. Every time I called her—which was often—she was very inspiring to me. She would tell me really powerful things that helped my state of mind.

Aunty Lena moved from St. Lucia to New York City as a teenager in the 1960s. There she got involved in the Civil Rights movement, participating in marches against the wishes of her mother, who wanted her to remain on the straight and narrow. When Aunty Lena and I spoke on the phone, she would listen to my struggles in the SAWP and tell me about her own history of fighting racism and oppression. She talked a lot about the Civil Rights movement and its hard-won victories. These conversations were comforting, but they also were very relevant to what I was experiencing as a migrant worker. Not only did I see some connections between the oppression of African Americans and that of migrant workers in Canada, but I also realized that the path to justice required activism and organization. These conversations helped to plant the seeds of activism in me.

So in my early days, these were the significant people who helped me during my "teething period" in the farm program. The One Love group, my niece in Brampton, and my aunt in the United States were the people who held my hand and guided me through those early rough waters.

Chapter 14
FAMILY SEPARATION

Being a migrant farm worker means that you are in a foreign country, away from your family, away from your friends, away from the community that you grew up in. You're in a new country, a different culture, and the hardest part of it all is being away from your family. To be away from your family for up to eight months of the year means that there will be a lot of changes in your community while you are away. Some people will die. There will be sad news as well as good news, all happening in your absence.

Especially difficult—even inhumane—is being separated from your children for eight months at a time. Being isolated on the farm, sometimes with limited communication, it was difficult to deal with all that. My children and their well-being was a constant source of worry while I was in Canada. And when I went back home, it could be difficult to catch up with all the news and changes.

When I first came to Canada in 2012, my daughter was eleven and my son was thirteen. It was the first time that I would be away for so long from my family. My children were already without their mom, Diana, who had passed away in 2005 when they were four and six. I, the next person in line, was now moving away from them for such a long time and to a country so far away. The program does not allow you to bring your family nor allow you time to go visit during the contract period.

Family is everything. What is the purpose of life, if not to spend time and share with the people you love and who love you? Family is the building block of our society. We all strive to make sure that our family's future is better than the one we experienced. And that's why I came to work in Canada. But it didn't feel like a free choice. The discontents of my economic situation pushed me and I felt like I had no other choice but to join the program, even if it came at great cost to my family.

Migrant workers always ask the question, When is the best time to be away from your kids? The answer, of course, is that there is no best time. But I think that pre-teenage to teenage are some of the most difficult times to leave. There's so much that you miss at that critical stage of their lives. It's like they've slipped through your fingers. The question I always ask is: The damage that has been done, can it ever be repaired? That is the reality I'm facing now. Being away from your family is the heaviest price, the greatest injustice that migrant workers face wherever they are.

There is no reason why migrant workers—whether farm workers or live-in caregivers, who raise the children of their wealthy employers while separated from their own—need to be so strictly separated from their families. Instead, it is a *choice* made by power holders to structure temporary foreign worker programs in this way—yet another echo of slavery and yet another way in which migrant workers are destabilized, putting them in a position where it is almost impossible to fight back.

A common term in the Caribbean to describe the children of overseas migrant workers is "Barrel Babies," referring to the barrels full of presents and goods that workers ship home at the end of the season. You might say that migrant workers send *presents* in place of their *presence*. The absence of parents in the lives of their children results in untold damage. These were big challenges for me and for many of my co-workers as well, and I am still dealing with the aftermath.

The challenges of communication made things even more difficult. Phone cards would advertise one hundred or two hundred minutes, but that was for calls to the United States. Calling St. Lucia, with all the connection fees deducted, we might get only three or four minutes for a phone card that cost between $2.50 and $5. What kind of conversation can you have in four minutes? But what else can you do? It is expensive to make calls using calling cards.

My net pay did not allow me to cover all my expenses. I couldn't save. I was operating on a very tight spending plan. This was even more true since 25 percent of my weekly wages was withheld by the Eastern Caribbean liaison service as part of the compulsory savings scheme. Officials boasted that this scheme was of great benefit to migrant workers, their families, and the home country. But in reality, the scheme didn't quite deliver on these promises and caused a lot of stress for workers: there were many deductions taken from the forced savings, and the government was often very late in transferring workers' savings to them. (For example, after one of my seasons in Canada, I didn't receive my savings until more than four months after I had returned home; by that point, I was back in Canada again for the next season.)

The real reason for the compulsory savings scheme is to make sure that you return home after your contract, since you do not receive the money otherwise. This serves the interests of both Canada and the home countries, who do not want to lose the injection of foreign currency that migrant workers bring home each year. On the Canadian side, it's part of the broader policy of making sure that temporary foreign workers remain just that: temporary.

One funny story shows how deceptive phone cards could be. During my first year, a roommate of mine named Ted purchased a phone card that promised 240 minutes of calling time to the United States. Making a call to the US, Ted brought along a chair to settle down for a long conversation. To his total surprise, the phone card lasted less than half an hour. After he got over his initial disappointment, Ted's experience became a running joke, as we tried to figure out the rate of conversion between phone card time and actual time.

Along with being on a farm without internet, this is a recipe for your children to slip through. So when you put all of that together, you end up with a vicious cycle. You see, the program makes you dependent. You earn minimum wage and then have all these deductions—for your airfare, work visa, uniform, start-of-season loan, and bunkhouse utilities, in addition to all the usual taxes. So in eight months, it is like you only make four months' worth of wages. Then once you're back home, you have to stretch it. And you might not be able to find work for only four months. This then means that you have to go back to Canada again and go through the same thing. This all results in being dependent on the program.

The vicious cycle operates in other ways too. I came to Canada to better the lives of my children, but it resulted in me being locked out of their lives. They came to see me as a stranger. They also suffered in other ways. One place where their struggles began to show up was in their performance at school.

From the time I joined the program, my children's academic performance suffered, and they also began to have more behavioural issues at school and at home. All at once, they were dealing with the loss of their mother and the absence of their father while I was away on the program, all while living in a community (Belmont) that struggled with poverty and the social ills that come with it. I was constantly worried that my children could come under some of those negative influences. I came to Canada to graduate from the vicious cycle of poverty and social ills of Belmont, but I found my children and myself trapped deeper in that vicious cycle.

Being a migrant farm worker in Canada was a major challenge for me every day. It was like fighting two wars at the same time. On the one hand, I was fighting for better working and living conditions. On the other hand, I was extremely worried about my children back home.

My mental state wasn't one of hope and optimism; it was always a state of worry and fear. And at the same time, I was burdened with the desire to please my employer by whatever means possible.

◇◇◇

While I was in Canada I would see or hear about interesting places such as Niagara Falls, national or provincial parks, and beaches and think that they would be great places to take my children. Just ten kilometres south of Leamington, for example, is Point Pelee National Park, a protected peninsula with marshland, beaches, hiking trails, and canoes and kayaks for rent, where you can see nearly four hundred species of birds and witness the migration of monarch butterflies each fall. Many of the parks have wonderful activities for children that are both fun and educational—something that is largely absent in St. Lucia, unless you are wealthy or a tourist. Every time I would see those places I would ask: Why are my children not here? Why can't they be part of this?

Canada is known to be very family oriented. But as a migrant farm worker, being in Canada means being ripped away from your family. The best days for many parents in Canada—Mother's Day, Father's Day, Family Day—are migrant farm workers' worst days.

Chapter 15
BACK AND FORTH

One important part of being in the farm worker program is the experience of going back and forth between Canada and your home country each and every year. The S in the SAWP, of course, stands for "seasonal," meaning that we are only in Canada for a limited period of time. For some people, the season is as short as six weeks. These are generally workers who come to the apple orchards for harvesting. On the other end of the spectrum, some people's contracts, especially for those working in greenhouses, are for as long as eight months, like mine was. No matter how long your contract is, when you're on the SAWP, you're constantly going back and forth. By December 15 of each year, every SAWP worker needs to have left Canada.

It was always a joy to be reunited with my children after a long eight months in Canada and to see family and friends. These are the sweetest joys for migrant farm workers. But returning home each year brings difficulties as well.

For those of us on longer contracts, in our home countries, they see us as tourists. We're only back home for four months, and they see us like we are on vacation. They also have the impression that once you go to Canada, you're going to greener pastures. They don't hear about our troubles, so it's greener pastures. So when we go back home, people assume we have a good life, that we had a good season, that everything is good.

This can sometimes come along with unrealistic expectations. For example, people often think that if someone from their community is on the program then perhaps they could secure a spot for their son or brother or cousin. They see the program as an opportunity for easy employment and as a way out, and they don't realize that we don't have the power to recruit or nominate anyone.

Many people will also ask for money or other things. Unemployment is high, and some people have difficulty paying their bills or covering the cost of their children's education. They figure that with the wages you are earning in Canada, you can easily help out. Of course, it's not always possible for us to help. This can be a really difficult thing to negotiate, not meeting the expectations of your family, friends, and neighbours. Sometimes this can lead to people saying negative things, like that you are cheap or selfish, and can result in strained relationships.

The truth is that we do try to live up to expectations and share some of the modest wealth that we earn in Canada. A big way we do this is by bringing home a barrel stuffed with gifts.

◇◇◇

Migrating for work is a historic practice in my community—and throughout the Caribbean. Typically, when migrants returned home, either to stay or to visit, they brought with them gifts to treat their families and friends. With time, this has taken root and is now an important part of our culture. In our culture, returning home from overseas without gifts is like coming home on payday empty-handed. It is an obligation that all workers take seriously.

Collecting items for our barrels was a marathon that spanned several months. We had to monitor the ads for sales, especially for and during major events on the calendar like Mother's Day (generally for household items) and Father's Day (especially for tools and equipment). We also took advantage of the long day lengths of summer to use our bicycles to go and see deals that may be available at the garage and yard sales that are so common at that time of the year.

Shipping a barrel is a long process with lots of costs all over the place. An empty barrel—usually a large drum, either cardboard or blue plastic, similar in size to an oil drum—in 2014 cost $50 for a small and $60 for a jumbo. The cost of filling up a barrel varies from $500 to over $1,000. The cost of shipping that barrel to St. Lucia (by sea) was $60 for the small and $75 for a jumbo. After a month, we would be informed by way of a phone call from the shipping agent in St. Lucia that the barrel had arrived. A further fee is paid to the shipping agent for the paperwork to be presented to customs for the process of clearing, which entails inspection prior to paying duties. The final expense comes with the cost of transporting the barrel to its final destination, which varies depending on the distance from the point of pickup, or the port.

For those of us who are not new to the program, we would have a very long list of requests from our families and friends that would include things like the latest phones, brand name shoes, car stereos, and even the impossible, such as deer horns, an essential item in traditional medicine. My gifts were mostly clothing, household items, tools, and small appliances.

In a way, by bringing back all these gifts, workers are trying to demonstrate that things are going well on the program and that they are making a good living. This has the effect of making people expect gifts from returning migrant workers. Generally, farm workers don't talk about the hardships that they face. They'd rather that the gifts do the talking. Nobody talks about the hardships, the sacrifices they made to bring those gifts.

Gift giving can sometimes create rifts, with people asking why they didn't get a certain gift, or why they got something different than the next person. But even if gift giving can sometimes be a source of stress, I still did take a lot of pleasure in carrying out the practice. Here are my three favourite stories of gift sharing:

Roy: Roy went by many names and was many things to many people. These things went together: his many names and roles. Roy loved being called "Fever," in both English and Creole. When he was called "Roy Rogers," he would answer, "King of cowboys." Roy was a traditional fisherman and herbalist. He was a storyteller, a hunter, and, my favourite, he was a comedian. I gave Roy several gifts over the four years that I spent on the program. The gift that changed my relationship and attitude towards Roy was the day that I handed him a hunting knife that had a file (that always kept it sharpened) fitted in its casing, along with a backpack that allowed him to carry all his essentials for his adventures. Up to this day, Roy is still thankful for such treasured items. He behaves as if he got these items on hire purchase from me, and every time that he sees me, he must make an instalment of food and other goodies.

My half-brother Stephen, a.k.a. "Coolie-man": The day I handed Stephen a bread machine was the day our relationship took to a new level. He couldn't contain his amazement and deep satisfaction for such a small but mesmerizing piece of equipment that could mix and knead dough and even cook it all in one go. Ever since, he has told me that he can't stop eating bread, that this piece of equipment has renewed his appetite for bread. Our conversations always end with "Man does not live by bread alone," followed by a laugh.

Little Bryan: Bryan was a toddler from Belmont, from a family of eight or nine. The mom and the household were struggling to make ends meet. Up to this point, I hadn't had any personal encounter with Bryan, only with his mom and older siblings, especially Larry and Zacky. Bryan was too young to go down the steep flight of stairs which connected their home to their small front yard and the nearby road, our common meeting area.

One night after returning from Canada, I came to deliver some clothing items for the kids. These were clothes that I bought at a yard sale in Kingsville—the next town west of Leamington and another important agricultural centre—at a ridiculously low, even giveaway price.

The kids did not delay in trying on the clothing that I came to deliver to them. There was a black pair of shoes that fit Bryan perfectly. The shoes lit up in the dark every time Bryan took a step. To my surprise, Bryan started running back and forth, shaking their fragile-looking wooden home, and shouting out my name at the top of his voice.

That was a first for me. It was the first time I think someone ever shouted my name so loudly, all in joy. That was my very first encounter with Bryan. I was even more surprised that he knew my name. I had no idea that such a small item could instantly transform the world of a child. To this day, Bryan and I share a strong bond that was created that day. The memory of that moment is a permanent treasure of mine, one that I cherish alongside memories of my brother Victor, the only person who captured my heart in such a powerful way during my early, formative years. The memory makes me smile every moment I think about it. It raises my vibrational energy to a level that very few things can.

The priceless feelings I got from giving gifts like these I see as a major success of my time on the farm program.

◇◇◇

A final bright spot of my return home each year was seeing my friend Sharna. Sharna and I first met in the mid-2000s, when I was working for a bank as an agricultural credit officer and she was the receptionist for a small business that was a client of the bank. Every time I called or visited the client, I would have to go through Sharna.

We hit it off quickly and enjoyed each other's conversation. Although there was definitely a spark, our timelines did not yet align, and we became good friends rather than getting romantically involved. We remained quite close into my years on the SAWP, and I always looked forward to seeing her, connecting and catching up when I returned home from Canada. The spark was still there but we remained friends. Our timelines still did not align—yet.

Chapter 16
LITERACY AND POWER

One thing I noticed during my first year on the program was that most participants have very low levels of literacy. Many are functionally illiterate. So my education really stood out.

My first glimpse of this came during our flight to Canada, when many of my colleagues asked me for help filling out the immigration form on the airplane. Throughout the season, I continued to be called on to help colleagues with reading and writing—everything from interpreting letters from Canadian government agencies about social insurance cards or taxes to helping to write messages on WhatsApp or Facebook Messenger.

Workers' lack of literacy comes into play even before leaving for Canada. Notably, for workers with poor reading and writing skills, it is nearly impossible to understand the contract they have to sign. This is true even for workers from countries where English is the official language. In St. Lucia, the fact that Creole is the common spoken language makes comprehending the contract a special challenge for workers. And of course, as I described earlier, even if workers could read the contract, we are not usually given any time to do so before being pressured to "sign here."

My level of education made me an unusual participant in the program. Most guys had not enrolled in secondary school. Some of my co-workers asked, Why would a guy with that level of education be on the program? They simply could not wrap their heads around it. In St. Lucia, farm work was considered to be "low-skilled" and performed by people with little or no education. Of course, I had a different idea of agriculture, which had long been my passion. And my dire economic situation made the SAWP a financially attractive option, even with my level of education.

Most guys were grateful for the help I was able to give them with reading and writing. One thing people really appreciated was my confidentiality. Helping people with personal messages and government correspondence meant that I saw a lot of private information about their lives. But they never heard any of this information repeated around the farm, so they knew that I was maintaining that confidentiality. They really appreciated that. For me, having worked for a bank for five years as an agricultural credit officer, the principle of confidentiality had been drilled into me, and it was no challenge for me to maintain that level of trust.

Out of the blue, one Jamaican guy started to call me "Teacher." A handful of other Jamaicans began to call me that too. This group kept me on my toes with questions about our working conditions, St. Lucian culture, and some other general questions. They pushed me to learn more about the program at a time when I had still been thinking that because it was legal it was also just, even if some red flags had already begun to pop up. In this way, my "students" helped push me towards becoming an activist for migrant workers' rights in Canada.

◇◇◇

Later on, as I got to know a little more about the SAWP, I realized how low literacy was part of the broader design of the program, which ensures that workers are exploitable. The program is calling for people of colour. The program is calling for people who are illiterate, or who are struggling with English, or who have English as a second language. The program is calling for people who are largely ignorant about labour issues and human rights issues. These are the kinds of people that the program is really calling for—people who are easily exploited. To me, this was the slavery and colonial handbook being used in modern Canada, with power holders keeping labourers uneducated, poor, and unstable, and taking advantage of these conditions to exploit them and make a handsome profit.

True to this pattern, I noticed that most of my colleagues were very passive and bent on pleasing the employer. This was not surprising, since the threat of deportation was always hanging over our heads. When you're on the program, you never know where you stand. You don't know if you will be asked back by the employer for the next season. So in all of our actions, pleasing the employer was foremost. Speaking up meant standing the risk of being sent back home.

Truly, fear is woven into every aspect of the program. The SAWP is an employer-driven program. The imbalance of power is staggering.

It's not that my colleagues didn't have complaints. In the absence of the employer or authority, you would hear about their issues. But only in the absence of the employer. The constant threat of deportation—or of not being asked back to the farm the next year—made workers too afraid to bring complaints to the employer, even as a group. They would have preferred to have someone who could act as their delegate with the boss, but of course, no one wanted to volunteer for a job that would make them the sacrificial lamb. We were sandwiched between a rock and a hard place. If we spoke up to try to improve conditions on the farm, we risked being sent home to face high levels of unemployment and other very challenging economic conditions. Our extremely difficult and precarious situation forced us to be submissive and compliant.

Chapter 17
COPING AND FINDING COMMUNITY

With all the difficulties of being away from our families and the other countless challenges of being in the program, my colleagues and I had to find ways to cope with our situation, to make it through our eight months in Canada.

Socializing with other migrant workers, including from other farms, was an important way that people coped. Our bunkhouse was very popular. There were always visitors, especially on weekends, from other farms and from the wider community. Starting sometime during the summer, Friday began to be treated as the happy start to the weekend, even though we still had a full workday on Saturdays (and during my first year, on Sundays too). Friday was payday and also the day we would go into town to buy groceries, send money home, and run other errands. After shopping, drinking, dancing, and partying were the highlights of a typical Friday evening.

It was a common practice—almost a part of our culture—for us workers to treat ourselves on Fridays. Some treated themselves with drinks, others with pizza, others with a barbecued whole chicken, and so on. (These weekend activities only really took off in summer because that was the point by which we had reached the halfway mark of our contracts and paid off advances for our airfare and start-up loans. From this point, the countdown to returning home was on.)

Even though starting the weekend festivities on Friday might mean being tired at work the following day, it was important to us to have a few evenings of socializing and blowing off steam. On Saturdays, we would work a full day, but as soon as work ended, the lively weekend activities resumed. The music on Fridays, Saturdays—and often enough on Sundays—was always very loud and went late into the night.

The music selection covered a wide range, from politically conscious reggae to love songs and pure West Indian party music.

After I left the farm in 2015, Sunday also became the day for cricket matches. Guys would invite workers from other farms to come join in, so this, too, became a big social event. Other sports and games—soccer and dominoes, for example—were also popular ways to pass the time.

There was always something to celebrate in the bunkhouse: birthdays, St. Lucian holidays, and other occasions. To outsiders, we were merrymakers. Of course, there were also moments throughout the season when colleagues would receive bad news from back home, which could bring down the mood of the entire bunkhouse. And as I mentioned before, certain holidays, such as Mother's Day, Father's Day, and Family Day, were bittersweet—usually more bitter than sweet.

In many ways, all these social activities were just ways of coping with family separation and other stresses. People also coped by taking a bike ride to town to purchase items on sale, or taking day trips to the big cities of Toronto or Windsor or somewhere else. A lot of us on the farm would have a friend or relative who lived in Toronto who would come visit and occasionally pick us up and take us to Toronto to shop or attend events like Caribana (the city's annual celebration of Caribbean culture, featuring street parties and mas bands). This was only possible when we had a day off. These were outings that guys really looked forward to. Bradley (a.k.a. "Chow"), Mike, and Martin were regular visitors to our farm from Toronto. Martin was not only a regular visitor, but he even camped out by our bunkhouse with his family on the weekends he came to visit.

Alcohol and smoking were other things that guys did to get through their time in Canada. Some guys used it to socialize and have fun, but there were others who obviously had no control. Sometimes people would fall asleep or vomit in the bunkhouse's common area on Sundays. In extreme cases, someone might get so sick that they would have to skip work on Monday. Drugs and gambling were other forms of coping that could also cross the line into abuse.

As for me, I used a combination of things to cope with my situation. Along with my colleagues, I really enjoyed watching wrestling on TV. Wrestling was like our soap opera. We spent a lot of time dwelling on the events of the last episode and speculating as we eagerly looked forward to the next one.

To my surprise, an important place where I found community—and that helped me cope with everything—was a church in Leamington. As I have mentioned, churchgoing was something I had not practised for many years before I joined the program. Even holding a Bible had become difficult for me. The complicity of organized religion—and the Catholic Church in particular—in colonialism and slavery, and its role in suppressing grassroots political action made me turn my back on religion.

As I've said, in my first months in the program, we worked Sunday to Sunday, with no rest day. But later on, starting late in my first or early in my second year, Sunday became a rest day, and I began to attend the Leamington Gospel Hall. The way it happened was that a co-worker named Thompson, a.k.a. "Indian," knew a Canadian missionary from Sarnia who had started a church in Forestiere, St. Lucia. Thompson was an active member of that church, so when he came to Canada, he connected with the missionary, who told him about a branch of the same church in Leamington. Thompson began to attend, and he also paid great attention to the sixteen of us newcomers. He made it his duty to invite everyone to church.

When I came to Canada in 2012, I could not see myself holding a Bible or going to church. But being on an isolated farm, not integrated into society, away from friends and family, I was looking for ways to cope with the situation that were healthier than drinking or smoking. (I am a social drinker but had no interest in becoming dependent.) One alternative activity was church. So even though I had long-held objections to organized Christianity, my desire for a constructive social activity—combined with my curiosity to witness a new church in this new country—led me to finally accept Thompson's invitation and attend a service at the Leamington Gospel Hall.

Aside from about ten migrant workers, the small congregation of less than a hundred was all white—but we received a very warm welcome. Even though it had been difficult for me to bring myself back into a church building, once I got to know the Leamington Gospel Hall a bit, my decision to choose church over some of the other coping strategies was firm. But it didn't mean that I gave up my reservations about organized Christianity. To this day, I am still of the opinion that Christianity encourages obedience and subservience.

But my desire for a healthy social activity outweighed all of those concerns, and I looked forward each week to attending church, even if I didn't agree with much that was said from the pulpit. Indeed, at the Leamington Gospel Hall, I came face to face with some of the greatest people, who were compassionate and understanding. A few people who really stick out in my memory were Jim, John, Abe, and the pastor Bruce Cottrill, who were all extremely welcoming, warm, friendly, and loving. That made all the difference.

Once a month, the church would have a potluck. Each church member would bring a contribution, and everybody would share the meal. That was an opportunity for us to socialize with the other members of the congregation. The food was very different to what we were accustomed to. But there was no doubt that it was a balanced meal served with love. On Sundays when there wasn't a potluck, Jim or one of the other parishioners would take us to their home for a family meal.

Two children also stand out in my memory of the church. The first was a boy of five or so named Ian, who was Jim's grandson. We formed a really strong bond. He was very full of energy and playful, and the moment he would spot me in the crowd, he would drop what he was doing, run towards me with his arms wide open, and jump on me. He would say, "I miss you." That just blew my mind every time. Being so far from my children made these moments very special. I would look forward to seeing Ian in church every Sunday. There could be a million people in the church, but if Ian wasn't there, it seemed empty to me. To this day, we have a strong bond.

The other child who I remember especially fondly was Curtis. Curtis had a disability and had difficulty walking and slurred speech. I believe he was also hard of hearing and had reduced vision. The things that stimulated him were sometimes surprising. For example, if someone dropped something on the floor and it made a loud noise, while everyone else would flinch, Curtis would laugh. It was a challenge to get him to laugh in other ways. I developed a strong bond with him and that was powerful. I would sometimes drop things on the floor to make Curtis laugh. Giving him a squeeze right above his knee made him laugh too. Or I would help him to say his name. This would also make him laugh. Seeing the smiles on Curtis's and Ian's faces would make my day.

Joining the church also enabled me to see a bit more of Ontario. Sometimes church groups would go out to various towns and cities to evangelize or attend religious meetings or events. I was able to come along a few times when a group was going to Windsor to participate in Christian events held at the University of Windsor. I did find it ironic to go to a university campus, when my work permit forbade me from enrolling in educational programs. But this gave me the chance to see Windsor, the closest city to Leamington, just fifty kilometres away. Of course, we left after work and this was during the winter, so I only saw Windsor at night. But I was quite impressed to see the bright lights coming across the river from Detroit, and the busy Ambassador Bridge that connects the two cities.

Even though I didn't see a whole lot of the city, just the fact of going somewhere different was a form of coping for me. Because otherwise I would never get the opportunity to go to Windsor or anywhere outside the immediate Leamington area. In this same way, I was able to visit some other places as well: for example, Sarnia and St. Thomas, two other cities in the region, each approximately 150 kilometres from Leamington.

◇◇◇

A major development that also helped me to cope with being so far from my family happened completely by accident. One Friday afternoon, after the end of the workday, as I was walking through Leamington completing my weekly errands, I came across a garage sale. The guy running the sale had quite a few tools that I thought would be useful to me and my friends back home.

I told him I was interested in the tools, but that since I didn't have enough money on me, I would have to come back. That same day was my turn to receive the susu lump sum from my roommates, so I had more than enough money—just not on me at the moment.

He was so nice. He introduced himself as Denis and told me that as long as I made a deposit, he would put the tools aside for me. Thinking I would need to make a significant deposit to reserve the $280 or so of tools I was interested in, I told him that I didn't have enough on me at the time. But Denis insisted that I could just give him *anything* and he would hold them for me.

I can't remember exactly how much I gave him, but it was less than $20—a tiny fraction of the total cost of the tools. But this was enough for Denis. He put the tools aside for me, and I came back for them later that evening.

That night, I did not just get a new set of tools. I also made a friend. And that friend opened up a whole new world for me. From then on, every Friday when I went to town for shopping day, I would stop off at Denis's for a visit.

My whole experience with Denis was like my windfall in Canada: he gave me meaningful gifts, introduced me to wonderful friends, and even provided the key that opened the door for me to gain status in Canada. These beautiful things happened to me when I least expected them.

One of the many treasured gifts that Denis gave me was a used radio cassette player. That kept me busy listening to inspirational and spiritual tapes, especially by Louise Hay. I found them to be extremely helpful. From them I learned the practice of recording three daily positives that were the highlights of my day. The discovery that there is always something to be thankful for was a major shift and coping technique for me.

Through Denis, I found my first "Canadian mom," his neighbour Tina, who treated me as her son. These two enjoyed my companionship and invited me over whenever my schedule allowed. They both showed me a side of Canada that I knew existed and that I keep yearning for, but which I never saw a hint of on the farm.

Denis also introduced other friends too—an Ontario Provincial Police (OPP) officer, a former Mountie, and others. Some of them were hunting buddies. They affectionately called Denis, who was originally from Quebec, "Frenchie."

These guys began inviting me and some of my co-workers to participate in all sorts of activities. The OPP officer invited us over to swim in his pool. Another guy invited us to share Thanksgiving dinner with his family. They took us to London, Windsor, and Pelee Island, an island in Lake Erie, a ninety-minute ferry ride south from Leamington.

One of the members of this friend group, Louis Zonta, from nearby Kingsville, became my "Canadian dad." Louis picked me up every weekend and took me to his home so that I could use the internet to connect with my family and friends. Louis also cooked a variety of Italian meals for me and two other guys from the farm, Jamie and Julius, a.k.a. "Buddy." Louis really cemented our friendship when he gave me a key to his house and told me that I was always welcome.

(The strange thing about my countless encounters with Louis is that the same ways that he consistently described and referred to me are the exact ways that I would and should describe his love and commitment to me. "You are a godsend," "You are gold," and "You are a brother" are some of the things Louis says to me that echo exactly how I feel about him.)

Basically, this group of friends helped us integrate into the community. All of this was the result of that low deposit I paid at the garage sale that Friday.

Chapter 18
RACISM AND DISCRIMINATION

U nfortunately not all my experiences with Leamington residents were as friendly as those I had with Denis, Tina, Louis, and their friends. Being on the program meant dealing with all shades of racism and discrimination. On the farm we were mostly surrounded by fellow migrant workers, so incidents of discrimination were rare. It was in town where we sometimes ran into problems.

Friday evenings are the busiest time in Leamington. For most farms, Friday evening is shopping day. The streets and shops of Leamington are full of migrant workers, transported into town by buses arranged by their employers. Workers usually have just a couple hours to do all their errands for the week: sending money to our families back home and purchasing supplies for the week.

When workers did their weekly shopping at Leamington's super-markets, there would be really long lines at the cashiers, with workers pushing carts full of supplies for the coming week. Sometimes we would hear white customers grumbling about the long lines and com-plaining about us.

More overt racism also took place in town. On one shopping day, a distant cousin of mine—who was also working on the SAWP at the time, along with two of his brothers—was shopping at a popular supermarket in Leamington and was pulled aside by a security guard who made a very stereotypical racist accusation when he accused my cousin of not paying for his groceries. Even when my cousin showed his receipt, the security guard did not back down and continued to question him. All of this happened in a crowded store and was a humiliating experience. He eventually sued the store over the incident, and the case was settled out of court.

Probably every single migrant farm worker in Leamington has experienced racist or discriminatory verbal abuse at one time or another. Personally I had a number of experiences while cycling when people in passing cars would yell things at me as they drove by—sometimes dangerously close to me. I couldn't always make out exactly what they said, but sometimes would hear them yell, "Go home!" During the summer this would happen about once a month. Often enough, in the bunkhouse, colleagues shared their own stories of encountering racism at work or in the community.

◇◇◇

One especially outrageous incident of racism in the community came in 2013 when about one hundred Caribbean migrant workers in Elgin County were subjected to a "voluntary" DNA sweep after a woman reported being sexually assaulted by a migrant worker. The description of the suspect was of a Black man, between five foot ten and six feet tall. But for the Elgin detachment of the Ontario Provincial Police, who were working the case, all that seemed to matter was that he was Black. Officers went to the farm closest to the assault and asked workers to provide DNA samples that could be tested against the crime scene evidence. They later expanded the DNA sweep to four more farms in the area, collecting a total of 96 DNA samples.

Despite the victim's description of her attacker, police collected samples from men ranging in height from five foot two to six foot six, and in age from twenty-two to sixty-eight years old. Given the profound power imbalances within the SAWP, workers did not feel that participating in the DNA testing was truly "voluntary." They worried that by not participating in the sweep they could be jeopardizing their future employment in Canada. And they turned out to be 100 percent correct about that: three workers on one farm who refused to participate were not requested back by the employer the next season for that exact reason, as the employer himself explained to the OPP in a letter that was part of the evidence for the case.

Fifty-four of the affected workers took the OPP to the Human Rights Tribunal of Ontario over the incident. Jamaican Logan Leon, the lead plaintiff in the case, voiced some of the workers' complaints: "I didn't have a choice," he explained. "If I said no, I don't know what [would] happen." The experience made Leon feel "sad, defeated, and humiliated."[33]

In August 2022, the Tribunal found in favour of the workers, ruling that the OPP had discriminated against them on the basis of race, skin colour, and place of origin. Each affected worker will be offered $7,500 in damages. (By the way, the sweep did not succeed in identifying the actual assailant, who refused to participate, but was not one of the three men I mentioned above).

◇◇◇

Workers also experience racism at work. In 2009, a fellow St. Lucian, Adrian Monrose, was working at a greenhouse operation, Double Diamond Acres, in Kingsville, Ontario. On at least two occasions, the co-owner of the greenhouse called Monrose and fellow Caribbean workers "monkeys." After Monrose complained about this racist abuse, he was fired and sent back home to St. Lucia. Monrose took Double Diamond to court, filing a complaint with the Human Rights Tribunal of Ontario. In 2013, the Tribunal finally reached its decision and found in Monrose's favour, ordering Double Diamond to pay him $23,500 in lost wages and other damages.[34]

Another place where I noticed discrimination and hypocrisy is in how workers who break their contracts and leave their farms are treated. During my four years on the program, three fellow St. Lucians from my bunkhouse walked away from the program to remain in Canada without legal immigration status. In the eyes of the government—and some Canadians—these men became "illegal immigrants" and were all of a sudden seen as criminals. I find it highly ironic that a country that takes pride in its history as a refuge for runaway slaves from the United States can have this reaction to workers fleeing such an oppressive migrant labour program.

Discrimination extended even to local politics in farm towns. In Leamington, residents have long complained about having so many migrant workers in town, especially on shopping days and weekends. The issue came to a head in 2017 when the Leamington Business Improvement Area (BIA) began to lobby the town council for a bylaw to prevent loitering. The BIA and their supporters thought that migrant workers were taking up too much space on the streets and preventing residents from accessing shops and enjoying the town. Though the bylaw was never formally proposed, many local politicians and residents agreed that "loitering" was a major problem. The mayor of Leamington at the time, John Paterson, also made comments that accused Caribbean—and in particular Jamaican—workers of engaging in sexual harassment. "Not to be bigoted, not to be racist, not to be anything, it is directly related to some of the Jamaican migrant workers that are here," said Paterson.[35]

Leamington is the tomato capital of Canada. Leamington is the greenhouse capital of Canada. And that status is entirely the result of the work of the ten thousand or more migrant workers who work in the Leamington area each year. For such a community to propose anti-loitering bylaws targeted at the migrant farm workers who are the engine of the town's economy is a bold statement from white supremacists.

One thing I found strange and disappointing is that migrant workers spend a significant amount of money in Leamington, and that money provides a big boost to local businesses and the economy. But when the anti-loitering bylaw was being discussed, I don't remember any of the businesses where migrant workers shopped saying anything in support of migrant workers or against the proposed bylaw. I don't remember the Chamber of Commerce speaking up either.

The town of Kingsville has also made efforts to keep migrant workers out of its downtown. In 2020, its town council passed a bylaw that placed limits on the housing of migrant workers off-farm. The bylaw stemmed from greenhouse operators renting accommodations for migrant workers in town, a situation that caused "some significant concerns," according to Kingsville mayor Nelson Santos.[36]

With both these bylaws (proposed or actual), the goal was to keep us isolated on the farm and to maintain racial purity in town, to keep the races on the farm, keep the streets clear of them, and keep the community all white. This was the work of white supremacy in action.

These incidents also show that the injustices that migrant workers face in Canada are at every level of government. The oppressive structure of the program is set at the federal level, and the labour laws that discriminate against farm workers are provincial. But migrant workers are even treated as second-class by the small towns where they work—and by some of the residents.

Migrant workers and activists fought back against these laws. A big rally was organized in Leamington by Justicia for Migrant Workers. By this time, I was living in Toronto and very involved with activist work. I attended the demonstration along with people from Toronto, London, Kitchener, Chatham, and Windsor. A number of unions and other organizations stood with us as well: the Canadian Union of Public Employees (CUPE); the Ontario Public Service Employees Union (OPSEU); the Industrial Workers of the World (IWW); the London and District Labour Council; the Ontario Secondary School Teachers' Federation (OSSTF); $15 and Fairness; and others.

Wearing a sign that read "Migrant Workers Are the Engine of the Tomato Capital," I addressed the rally and expressed the anger and frustration that migrant workers feel while living and working in the community, but not being valued as members of it. I told the rally that day, "If we are good enough to work here, we are good enough to do business here."

The loitering bylaw did not end up getting passed, but it was just one more example of the broader racism and discrimination that migrant workers often deal with in Canada.

Chapter 19

A VOICE FOR THE VOICELESS

During my first year, just a few weeks after I arrived in Canada, there was a major accident in Hampstead, Ontario, about thirty kilometres west of Kitchener-Waterloo. A van carrying thirteen poultry farm workers from Peru and Nicaragua back to the bunkhouse after a day's work collided with a flatbed truck at a rural intersection. It was a horrific crash. Ten of the farm workers and the Canadian truck driver died.

News reached the bunkhouse quickly. But what made this situation even more challenging was the fact that we didn't have many details about the accident. We were very concerned, especially those of us who were new to the program and now had death associated with migrant farm labour in Canada for the first time. Being that it was our first season, we had no idea how close or how far from us that accident was. Nor did we initially know which country the victims were from. We were concerned about whether we were at risk ourselves.

Later that year, in the summertime, my co-worker Vincent "Bois" Toussaint, who had been in the program for a few years, told me that a vigil was going to be held in Hampstead in honour of the crash victims. The vigil was being organized by Justicia for Migrant Workers. This was the first time I had heard about this group. Bois asked if I was interested in attending and I said, "Yes, why not?" Transportation was being provided by the organizers for workers coming from Leamington. The vigil was being held on a Sunday, and by chance we had that Sunday off work when normally we worked seven days a week.

On the Sunday we were picked up in a school bus that stopped en route in Chatham and many other places to pick up more farm workers and people who wanted to attend. A diverse group of people were at the vigil: a handful of farm workers from different countries, working in different parts of Ontario; representatives from unions and activist groups; musicians; many Latin Americans; and people from many other backgrounds. Noticeably absent were the politicians and policy makers, farmers, and mainstream media. The very small turnout of migrant farm workers also stood out to me, but it wasn't all that surprising, since workers are often busy on Sunday preparing for the week ahead, cooking, doing laundry, shopping, and so on. Not to mention the fear of reprisal for participating in anything that could appear political.

During the vigil, various speakers talked about the harsh conditions that the crash victims and other migrant workers face. They argued that the accident could have been prevented, describing how the workers had worked very long hours with very little rest before the accident. The speakers explained how the structure of temporary foreign worker programs create the conditions to allow such abuses to take place and that tragedies like this would continue to happen if big changes weren't made. That was disturbing.

A migrant farm worker from Jamaica, who had lost part of his leg in a workplace accident and used crutches, also spoke to the rally. His testimony was very moving to me. Not only did he tell the story of his injury, but he was also very bold and clear about how the system is employer-driven and about the gross power imbalance in the program.

Other workers were invited to speak. On the spur of the moment, I decided that I would say a few words. It was the first time I had gotten an opportunity to vent my frustration about the program. I also realized that this was an opportunity, since the people at the vigil were those who were pushing for better conditions.

Another worker from my same farm, who I'll call Elijah, spoke before me. He presented things from his understanding of a Christian, biblical perspective, saying that we should obey our masters and that only a saviour could bring us the change that we are fighting for. As I've mentioned, that was a school of thought that I hadn't subscribed to for a long time. I was motivated to present a very different perspective from Elijah, and to speak about how *collective action* can bring change. About how our conditions are *human* made. Actually, I was happy that

Elijah spoke first because it helped clarify my own comments. I also felt a burning need to put forward a counter-argument, which helped calm my nerves.

My presentation was more radical and political, on the other end of the spectrum. I spoke about the big gap between what my expectations of the SAWP had been and what the reality was. And about how the Canada I had found as a migrant farm worker was not what I thought was the "real" Canada—it was not how Canada portrays itself and did not reflect a modern country. I was nervous about speaking because I was unprepared. There is a saying that defines success as when preparation meets with an opportunity. For me, an opportunity met me unprepared, in a foreign land, in front of an audience of strangers, on a program with so much fear woven into it. But Elijah's short talk was all the preparation time I had and needed, and it helped me to find the courage to speak in spite of my nervousness.

After the vigil, there was a lunch in Kitchener and we had a Skype call with one of the survivors of the crash, who was hospitalized and not doing very well. He spoke in Spanish and one of the organizers translated. As if he hadn't been through enough already, Canadian immigration authorities were trying to send him home to Peru even as he recovered in hospital. All of that was just mind-blowing to me.

◇◇◇

The Hampstead vigil was the first time I learned about J4MW and met some of the organizers, Chris Ramsaroop and Tzazná Miranda Leal. I realized that they are a voice for the voiceless. Just knowing that there were people who were aware of our difficult conditions was a big relief for me that day. Even better was learning that they were not an impromptu group and that the vigil was not a one-off activity, but that they were engaged for the long term. They were serious about connecting with workers and building trust. This knowledge helped me to cope with everything I was coming to realize about the program. Later on I would meet organizers from Justicia again when they came to Leamington to give workshops or touch base.

The organizers I met that day would become long-term colleagues over the years to come. Tzazná and Chris are great friends to migrant workers and champions of the workers' cause. Tzazná is very friendly. She was always checking up on us to see how we were doing and offering us help. She always kept us updated, invited us to events and meetings, and consulted with us. For his part, Chris is tireless. At events like these he is always working the room, speaking to everyone, finding out how informed workers are about their rights. Chris always wants workers to know about their rights and to be empowered. These were the two people who first and most enthusiastically pushed me towards activism in Canada.

That day was the beginning of my turn to activism in Canada. After that, I felt like I had a union fighting with me and for me. But becoming an activist wasn't a straight line for me—it wasn't something that was planned. And it was more of a marathon than a sprint. It continues to be a journey. A lot of things happened along the way, both things I experienced and stories that I read and heard.

Going back to my childhood, a lot of things I learned in and out of school helped shaped my thinking and prepared me for becoming an activist. I think, for example, about studying Caribbean history, about revolutions from the Haitian (1791–1804) to the Grenadian (1979). I also remember learning about the history of US intervention and aggression in the Americas, something that's still influencing policies throughout the hemisphere. These are things that really touched me and pushed me. My experiences working in the community in St. Lucia as a teacher, extension officer, and community worker also helped prepare me for my later turn to activism in Canada.

In Canada, I was touched not just by the Hampstead accident but also by everything else I had experienced and heard about from colleagues—the exploitation and abuse at work; the deplorable, eighteenth-century working and living conditions; the racism; the structure of the SAWP which keeps workers temporary and strongly discourages them from speaking out. I also learned about some of the more shameful chapters of Canadian history. I learned about Canada's long history of migrant labour arrangements that dehumanize and exploit people, going back to the days of Chinese railroad workers. I also learned about Canada's history of colonialism and its mistreatment and oppression of Indigenous peoples: residential schools, the Sixties Scoop, missing and murdered Indigenous women and girls.

All of this gave me a lot to think about and I spent much time deep in thought, in conversations with myself. I kept telling myself that regardless of what comes my way, I must survive, and that eventually better must come. And that I had the power to make it happen. I thought about other things I had read or learned. I thought about certain quotations like the words of Desmond Tutu, who said, "If you are neutral in situations of injustice, you have chosen the side of the oppressor." Another quotation I thought about came from Elie Wiesel, who said, "We must take sides. Neutrality helps the oppressor, never the victim. Silence encourages the tormentor, never the tormented."[37]

I also recalled the first political book that I had read, in 1993: *Helping Health Workers Learn: A Book of Methods, Aids and Ideas for Instructors at the Village Level* by David Werner and Bill Bower. I'd found the book completely by chance while browsing the shelves of the central library in Castries. The book's authors tell the story of three school dropouts—peasant boys—from Italy who were taught to read and write by a priest. The boys wrote: "Whoever is fond of the comfortable and fortunate stays out of politics. He does not want anything to change. . . . To get to know the children of the poor and to love politics are one and the same thing. You cannot love human beings who were marked by unjust laws and not work for other laws."[38]

How can you say you love people who are marked by unjust laws and not fight for better laws? This has always been relevant to me. In Canada, it certainly was a huge factor that pushed me to take action.

I used to think that when practices are legal it means that they are right and just. But now, finding myself in a totally legal yet deeply unjust migrant labour program, I had to ask myself: Just because something is legal, is it really right? Is it really just? I suppose I had forgotten that slavery, colonialism, and apartheid had all been perfectly legal systems in their day. Thinking this over, I then had to ask myself if I believed that a new, fairer, better world is possible and whether unjust laws can and must be changed. I reasoned that unjust laws are not natural laws; they are only human made. That was something I convinced myself of. And since they were human made, I became convinced that they can be changed. That was critical, believing that I was fighting a battle that could be won. And that doing nothing about the condition of migrant workers actually amounted to supporting it and allowing the situation to become worse.

These were critical reflections that pushed me to become an activist. I thought about the saying that things were created to be used; people were created to be loved. When things like profit are being loved, and people of colour are being used, exploited, and abused, you can either remain silent or become an activist. For me, the choice was clear.

When I think about the whole process of becoming an activist, I group it into two simple stages: awareness and empowerment. A key part of me becoming aware of the issues was my ability to read. I would also say that there is something inside of me that gives me a tendency to question the status quo, and sometimes to challenge it when it appears unjust. I also have a thirst for deeper knowledge about how the world works and how things came to be the way they are. All of that helped in that process of awareness, in awakening to reality.

The other part is empowerment. Gaining awareness of the facts helped to empower me. So did having a whole network of friends and colleagues and an organization like J4MW as a support network. That was important in becoming empowered to become an activist. The conversations I had with myself were also key to my empowerment. Through that inner journey, I gradually overcame my self-imposed fear of speaking out. Gaining more experience with public speaking also helped empower me over time.

Looking back at my working life, my worst working conditions were without a doubt under the SAWP. But as bad as those conditions were, something good came out of them. All that I endured and experienced during my four years on the program galvanized me to take action, to fight back against the profound injustices faced by migrant workers in Canada. I was also pushed by my family history: descending from both enslaved Africans and indentured Indians, and now finding myself trapped in yet another form of exploitative labour program, I felt driven to break that vicious cycle and pursue freedom. My gross dissatisfaction and burning desire to speak up pushed me to the point of fearlessness and led me to what I discovered to be my greatest passion, activism.

Part Three
STATUS FOR ALL

Chapter 20

THE TWENTY INJUSTICES OF CANADA

As I spent more and more time in the SAWP, I identified what I call the Twenty Injustices of Canada. These are the twenty difficult conditions that migrant workers face. I discovered that if you're a migrant farm worker in Canada, you will be isolated, made to feel invisible, work under exploitative conditions that are all legal, risk deportation if you speak up, and quite possibly suffer wage theft, racism, harassment, and deplorable living conditions, among other things. These injustices are perpetuated at every level of government, from the federal to the provincial to the local. We are denied fundamental human rights and basically dehumanized and exploited.

So many of these Twenty Injustices make me think about the conditions of enslaved Africans during the colonial period in the Caribbean (and elsewhere) and of the indentured labourers who came afterwards. My ancestors were part of each group. I often think about how even though slavery and indentured labour are in our past, the echoes of these institutions can still be heard, loud and clear, in our modern world. Canada's migrant labour system is one place where this is certainly the case. Thinking about this history, I can't help but notice that many of these injustices seem to be drawn from the handbooks of slavery and colonialism as highly effective strategies for keeping working people precarious, oppressed, and exploited.

Here are the Twenty Injustices:

1. **We have tied work permits.** Migrant workers' work permits tie us to our employer. To be tied to an employer with the power to deport you for speaking up is a recipe for exploitation. As the experts say, we are "unfree" workers.

2. **We can't apply for status (or rights).** In other words, it is nearly impossible for migrant workers to transition from a tied work permit to an open one. Having permanent immigration status would help us to access decent work with better conditions, and allow us to be united with our families. Not having status in Canada means being denied basic human rights and labour standards. It also means that migrant workers are an unstable population—and an unstable population can't fight back.

3. **Employers control our housing.** Our housing is typically overcrowded, substandard, and poorly regulated. We live in isolated homes on farms. Our employers are also our landlords. We are treated as property.

4. **We have no say in our contracts.** While Canadians might "thank a union" for the benefits of collective bargaining, we migrant farm workers have no say in the terms and conditions of our employment. The contracts are determined at annual meetings between government representatives from Canada and the participating countries. Workers have no seat at the table.

5. **The threat of deportation keeps us quiet.** At any time, for any reason, farmers can send us home, where unemployment is high and wages are lower than in Canada. Our employers even control the travel agency that books our flights in and out of Canada. The threat of deportation coerces migrant workers to work under dangerous conditions and discourages us from speaking up.

6. **The migrant labour system is racist from top to bottom.** The SAWP is based on the idea that some lives matter less—namely, the lives of Black and brown migrant workers from the Global South. Racial injustice is inherent to Canada's migrant farm labour system, which exploits the labour of racialized migrants to subsidize the lifestyle of a few, in a system where food is a commodity and not a basic human right. This racism trickles down from the structures of the program to the day-to-day experiences of migrant workers, who are subject to police harassment, slurs, verbal abuse, and

other forms of mistreatment in the communities where –since 1966—they have worked and lived for part of each year.

7. **We are denied overtime pay and often denied minimum wage.** Farm workers have a different set of employment laws and are denied basic labour standards. Workers in other sectors get overtime pay after working forty-four hours in a week. Migrant farm workers often work as much as eighty hours per week (or more), but do not get overtime pay for those hours. Paycheque deductions and a variable piece rate often bring workers' pay to below minimum wage.

8. **We work in dangerous jobs with very little or no protection.** Agriculture is one of the most dangerous sectors for workers, with the fourth-highest fatality rate out of all employment sectors in Canada. The absence of unions makes it all the more difficult to ensure safe working conditions. The constant threat of deportation and prospect of not being able to provide for our families coerce us to work under dangerous conditions.

9. **Medical repatriation.** Doing such dangerous, non-unionized work, injuries are common. But when migrant workers get injured on the job, it is a common practice to send us back home.

10. **There hasn't been a single inquest into work-related deaths of migrant farm workers in Canada.** Despite the fact that an average of two workers in the SAWP die each year and that inquests into workplace deaths in other sectors are common, there has never been an inquest into the death of a migrant farm worker.

11. **Employment laws exclude us and are not responsive to our needs.** Most of the protections in the *Employment Standards Act* (Ontario) do not apply to farm workers. The same is true in most other provinces as well.

12. **Employment laws and program regulations are not enforced.** Even the small number of protections that do apply to migrant

farm workers are often not enforced. For example, all workers in Ontario, including farm workers, have the right to refuse unsafe work. But the pressures on migrant workers to keep quiet discourage us from speaking up. In fact, there have been multiple documented cases of migrant workers being blacklisted from the program after complaining about conditions. Of course, they have no recourse.

13. **We pay into employment insurance but can't receive benefits.** In this way, it is legal for all stakeholders of the program, including the federal government, to milk migrant farm workers. That is what I call an "association of exploiters." Working eight months in Canada on minimum wage and then spending four months at home un-' or underemployed is tough. Not being able to access employment insurance ensures that we live at the margins of society.

14. **Family separation.** We are physically separated from our families because we do not have status and we cannot bring our families with us. This is the cause of so much stress, heartbreak, and family trouble. Family separation, in my opinion, is the single greatest injustice of Canada's migrant farm labour system.

15. **Unjust immigration and labour laws.** From the Chinese railroad workers to today, Canada continues to use unjust labour and immigration policies to deny migrant workers equality by denying them basic labour standards and human rights. In the past, many European immigrants were granted permanent status upon arrival to Canada along with land. Black and brown migrant farm workers have a very different experience. Unjust labour and immigration laws and policies work in tandem to keep migrant workers vulnerable and precarious.

16. **We have to pay to work in Canada.** Migrant workers have deductions from our pay for airfare, a work permit, utilities, employment insurance that we can't benefit from, and sometimes other costs. All of this brings our take-home pay to below

minimum wage. Essentially it means that we have to pay for the privilege of working in Canada, even though we are here to do the dirty, difficult, dangerous, and non-unionized jobs that Canadians do not want to do. It can be even worse for migrant workers outside the SAWP, who sometimes have to pay outrageous fees to recruiters to get jobs in Canada (upwards of $8,000, in many cases).

17. **Farm workers in Ontario are excluded from collective bargaining.** Farm workers are excluded from Ontario's *Labour Relations Act*, which sets out the rules for collective bargaining. The same is true in some other provinces as well. Not having the representation of a union is another human-made layer that makes us invisible, all adding to the recipe for exploitation.

18. **There is a stark power imbalance between employers and workers.** As many of the other injustices show, the SAWP is an employer-driven program, and migrant workers have very little power. Employers lobby and have a lot of sway with government, while migrant farm workers can't even vote.

19. **Up to now, the Government of Canada has not signed, ratified, or implemented the International Convention on the Protection of the Rights of All Migrant Workers and Members of Their Families.** On the world stage, Canada portrays itself as a leader, a champion on human rights issues, a place of refuge, and a place of great diversity and inclusivity. But quietly, Canada hides the eighteenth-century working conditions that persist in sectors like agriculture and exploit migrants from the Global South.

20. **Migrant farm workers' grassroots organizations are either not invited, not consulted, or paid to keep quiet.** There are a few grassroots organizations with and for migrant workers across Canada. Of these, Justicia for Migrant Workers is the most political that I know of. Our demand is status upon arrival for all migrant workers. We will not accept funds from anyone who wants to keep us quiet or control our work.

Now the question is: How do we fix these Twenty Injustices, which put migrant workers into a position where we are desperate, unstable, tired, coerced, trapped, dependent, and fearful, and which make it so that it's almost impossible to organize or fight back? How do we empower workers in a program where employers control every aspect of our lives? How do we change the SAWP? If we tried to address each injustice individually that would merely be a band-aid solution. Instead, we need to address them all together.

The one policy change that would address the largest number of these injustices is the demand of my organization, Justicia for Migrant Workers: *that all migrant workers receive permanent immigration status upon arrival in Canada.* This wouldn't solve every single problem. But it would allow workers to at least choose their employers, negotiate better wages and conditions, quit bad jobs, reunite with their families, and not live in fear of deportation. Status would be a two-edged sword that would take care of both our labour and immigration vulnerabilities. That is why, at every single rally we organize, you will see many signs with our central demand: Status for All!

Chapter 21
LEAVING THE PROGRAM

My dream of living permanently in Canada was first planted between 1986 and 1989, when I was completing my secondary school education at a school that was a gift to St. Lucia from the Government of Canada. During my studies there, I felt compelled to end up in Canada. To me, Canada was a pacesetter, a place of very high standards, second to none.

Of course, my opinions of Canada began to change quite rapidly once I began working on the SAWP. By 2014, my third year in the program, it was clear to me that neither my working nor my living conditions in the program were improving, nor were there signs that they would any time soon. The great pressures of family separation were weighing on me more and more. My discontents with the situation were growing and eventually got to the threshold where I felt compelled to take action.

Returning to St. Lucia was not a great option, financially speaking. The economy was still struggling in the aftermath of hurricane Tomas and the global financial crisis. The banana industry was still in steady decline after the disastrous WTO ruling in 1997 and the destruction of the Black Sigatoka crop disease that began in 2010.

Even though Canada had disappointed me in many ways, I felt the strong pull of life in a developed country, a land of opportunities— even if those opportunities came with problems. And so, sometime in 2014, I made up my mind that I would apply to become a permanent resident in Canada.

Becoming a permanent resident was a very long, costly, slow, and lonely process, full of uncertainty. There is no clear pathway to permanent residency for workers in the SAWP. In fact, it is almost impossible for SAWP workers to attain permanent residency. I was embarking on a road seldom travelled by migrant farm workers and thus was a trailblazer of sorts.

That journey actually began with the garage sale where I met my friend Denis ("Frenchie") in 2012. Frenchie gave me the special gift of a used radio cassette player. In 2012, everybody was listening to CDs and MP3 players, and I had this radio cassette player, which was a bit old-fashioned. But it came in extremely handy. Since we didn't have internet on the farm, I used the radio to listen to the news, a few radio programs, or music in my free time.

One morning in 2014 as I was listening to the radio, I heard a lawyer on the air talking about the four-in, four-out rule for temporary foreign workers. This was a regulation passed under Prime Minister Stephen Harper's Conservative government, which stated that non-seasonal temporary foreign workers could only work for four consecutive years in Canada. After this, they would need to leave the country and stay out for four years before becoming eligible to work here again—for another four-year period. To me, this was an extremely cruel policy. That caught my attention.

At that time, we migrant workers didn't know all the facts. Most importantly, we didn't realize that the rule did not apply to workers in the SAWP. We were all concerned, curious, and searching for answers about how this would impact us migrant farm workers. (A few days later, we called our liaison officer and received the good news that this regulation did not apply to us—only to temporary foreign workers on non-seasonal, usually two-year, contracts. Still, it had caught my attention.)

It was very relieving to hear this lawyer on the radio discussing the policy change. Her name was Maria Fernandes, from Windsor. For me, this was a case of hearing from the right person at the right time. It gave me the push that I needed to take action on my desire to apply for permanent residency. That was a critical moment for me, my turning point. I was galvanized into action. I told myself that if Maria Fernandes is good enough to be on the radio program, then she must be good enough to guide me towards applying for permanent residency. I quickly got her number and called her that same morning. I felt that was the opening I needed. That morning, I went to work with a new mindset. I was now on a mission to become a permanent resident.

So that's how my journey to applying for permanent residency began. It all stemmed from that garage sale in 2012. That old-fashioned radio cassette player turned out to be my door opener for becoming a permanent resident.

With Maria's help, I decided to apply for permanent residency on humanitarian and compassionate grounds (H&C). This is a route to permanent residency for people in exceptional cases who would not otherwise qualify. The lack of a pathway for SAWP workers to attain permanent residency meant that humanitarian and compassionate grounds was my only option, so I decided to give it a try. The grounds for my application was the simple truth that I have two children whose mother passed away in 2005 and that my work was taking me so far away from them. The H&C application takes into special consideration the interests of any children involved in the case. I submitted my application in June 2015.

The entire process had four stages: the first three each took nine months, and the last stage three months. So it was thirty months in total from the submission of my application to receiving my permanent residency card.

Stage one was to have the humanitarian grounds of my application approved. The second stage required medical examinations (for me and my children), character references, and a review of my financial records. The requirements for this stage were endless: family records, work and travel history, financial documentation, certificates of character, medical reports, letters of support, and more. Maria helped me by going through them with a fine-toothed comb. Nine months after that came the third stage, an interview with an immigration officer that confirmed second-stage approval. The fourth and final stage was to receive my permanent residency card, which happened in December 2017.

◇◇◇

There were all sorts of challenging moments throughout the process. One was having to plan around my tight work schedule in order to travel to Windsor (forty-five minutes each way) to meet with Maria. Another source of stress was the question of whether or not I should remain in Canada while awaiting a decision on my application. And then, of course, the waiting itself was nerve-racking.

The most personally hurtful moment during the application process was when a friend from Leamington, who was quite close to me and who had agreed to write a letter of support for my application, called me early the very next morning after agreeing to write the letter to tell me that she could no longer do it. She didn't give me a reason. This was very disturbing to me and had me worried for a few days. I was a little concerned about losing a letter that could strengthen my application, but much more importantly, I was worried about our friendship and whether I had done something to offend her. This was a source of anxiety during an already anxious time.

But that was an unusual situation, because for the most part I had overwhelming support from the community I had built in Leamington and beyond: from friends including Frenchie and the other friends I had met through him, organizations like J4MW and Inter Pares (a non-profit social justice organization that has been a staunch supporter of migrant workers in Canada), former Peace Corps volunteers who I knew from St. Lucia, and a few university professors. In addition to Maria, I received timely assistance from another immigration lawyer, the amazing and dynamic Karin Baqi. All my encounters with Karin have left me no other choice than to call her the bearer of good news. I also had the strong support of my extended family back home in St. Lucia.

Three examples of support from friends stood out. First, my "Canadian dad," Louis Zonta, signed an affidavit stating that he was responsible for me. That was huge. He also transported me to and from Windsor, allowing me to keep all my appointments with Maria to get my application completed and submitted. If not for him, I would have had to take a taxi, which cost about fifty dollars each way at that time.

Second, Steven Schroeter, a former Mountie who I met through Frenchie, wrote a letter of support that to this day is still deeply moving.

Third, Kade, a.k.a. "Parry," who worked with me on my beekeeping operation in St. Lucia and became my best friend, wrote a letter of support from his home in New York that was a pleasant shocker for me.

The agonizing process was finally completed when I received my permanent residency card in December 2017. This great milestone wasn't a cause for a big celebration, however, because I still did not have my children with me. Getting them to Canada would take another year and a half.

◇◇◇

I submitted my application for permanent residency in June 2015, and my contract at the greenhouse ended in September or October. I had to remain in Canada in order to be available for an immigration interview that could happen at any time. There were many complications during this transition from the SAWP to permanent residency status. A major one was that I was not allowed to work for the first nine months after my farm contract ended, nor was I eligible to apply for employment insurance, even though I'd been contributing to it for the last four years. This made my financial situation very precarious.

Another big challenge was that I found myself without health insurance for about nine months. Soon after my contract ended, I wasn't feeling well. Without giving it a second thought, I went to a walk-in clinic to see a doctor. My Ontario health card had an expiry date of December 15 (the last date by which SAWP workers need to exit the country), so I didn't think anything of going to the doctor. To my surprise, however, I learned at the clinic that my card had expired the same day that my contract ended. I was cut off from health care. This was my first hint of what life in Canada looks like without immigration status.

I could only apply for a new health card after the first stage of my immigration application had been approved, which happened in March 2016. But I would have to wait another ninety days from that date before my health coverage actually kicked in. So I was without health insurance for over nine months after leaving the farm program, regardless of the fact that I had been working and living in Canada, paying taxes, for eight months of the year, over the last four years.

After finishing my contract on the farm, I moved first to Toronto, where my friend Allan invited me to stay with him. Even though there were challenges, there were at least two good things about this time of transition from temporary to permanent resident. First, it gave me the opportunity to discover Ontario and especially my new home of Toronto. And second, it gave me all the time I needed to bring my activism to a new level, as I will describe in the next chapter.

In the years after leaving the program, I've done all sorts of work, mostly in Toronto, but elsewhere too. Here are some of the jobs I've had:

- Line worker in an industrial bakery
- Construction worker
- Production worker and custodian at a juice plant
- Upholsterer at a furniture manufacturer
- Plumber's apprentice
- Grocery warehouse worker
- Field and packhouse worker on an organic vegetable farm (close to Kitchener)
- Fish cleaner at a fish plant
- Line worker at a polyethylene (nylon, plastic) plant
- Furniture and appliance delivery person
- Life insurance agent

A major challenge with these jobs—and a reason why I changed jobs so frequently—was the difficulty of getting time off for my activist work. The one exception was at the organic farm, whose owner-operators are members of the progressive National Farmers Union, a farmers' organization that supports the just treatment of migrant workers and everyone along the food chain. I left this position at the point when my children were coming to join me in Canada, thinking that they would have more opportunities in Toronto.

My permanent residency application was a journey filled with lots of uncertainties, but it led to a beautiful destination. Armed with permanent residency, I finally had the rights and security that had been denied me as a migrant farm worker, making both my working and living conditions so difficult. Permanent residency heralded a new chapter of my life.

Chapter 22

JUSTICIA

T he work I did in my first years after leaving the program was mostly about putting food on the table. But my real passion, one I had discovered while working on the program, was activism. Immediately after my contract ended in 2015, I began to dedicate my life to fighting the injustices of migrant labour in Canada.

I carried out my activist work as part of Justicia for Migrant Workers, the group I had first encountered at the vigil for the victims of the Hampstead van crash. J4MW is a grassroots collective, consisting of farm workers and allies. We are not a union—we do not get membership dues. And of course, farm workers in Ontario are barred from formally unionizing anyway.

What do we do? First of all, and most importantly, J4MW does political work. How do we do that? We advocate and do outreach in what we call creative organizing; we connect with workers, educate the public, and ultimately pressure the politicians to change unjust immigration and labour laws, most importantly by granting migrant workers permanent status upon arrival.

We educate, inspire, motivate, and empower our members. We believe in letting workers speak for themselves. We also help our members with all the issues associated with being in a vulnerable and precarious situation. When migrant workers get sidelined, they need help with everything from housing to legal advice, health, and transportation.

What are the demands of J4MW? Our central demand, again, is *permanent status upon arrival.* Anything less is simply a band-aid, temporary fix. It is important to stress that our demand is status *upon arrival* and not a "pathway" to permanent residency. The live-in caregiver program was structured with a pathway to residency. In theory, caregivers could apply after two years of work. But the caregivers have always told us that the so-called pathway to permanent residency is a minefield. There are no guarantees, and you are reliant on your employer in order to actually secure status. It's an extremely precarious position. That is why we insist on status upon arrival.

It is also important to note that this wouldn't be anything new. Historically, immigrants from Europe arrived in Canada without real limits on their rights or immigration status. We are just asking to have the same treatment as those earlier groups of mostly white immigrants.

As an activist, I've travelled back to Leamington and to other agricultural towns countless times, conducting outreach to farms and often meeting with workers off-farm in creative organizing to protect the workers against the constant fear of reprisal and deportation. When we meet with workers, it's for a variety of reasons such as education (workshops), connecting and building trust (social activities and one-on-one conversations), and direct action (rallies, marches). We also regularly partner with our allies on a variety of matters such as health, legal information, immigration, and workplace injury and accidents.

Meeting with so many migrant workers, I constantly see the fear in their eyes, faces, words, tone of voice, and body language. When speaking to me one-on-one, they tell me about all sorts of abuses they are facing in their workplaces, but their precarious immigration status makes them too afraid to act. This always makes a big impression on me. So many workers are disappointed with the conditions they have found in Canada. I remember hearing some Mexican workers in one session say, "When the large countries sneeze, the small countries get sick." Other workers say things like, "We play fair, while others cheat."

A lot of my activist work has involved telling the story of migrant workers in Canada. I have probably spoken to close to one hundred audiences about migrant labour in the last seven years, since leaving the program. I've spoken to audiences ranging in size from under ten to over three hundred, all over Canada and the United States: across Ontario and in Quebec, Alberta, British Columbia, and Prince Edward Island; and in New York City, Chicago, New Mexico, Washington State, and Kalamazoo, Michigan. I've spoken at protests in the freezing cold, in comfortable hotel conference rooms, in university lecture halls, and online: some of my recorded talks are available on YouTube.[39]

I've spoken to students (from high school to undergraduate to postgraduate), churches, unions, and countless allies all along the food chain. In some settings I speak for as little as five minutes, in others as long as one hour, plus time for questions and answers. I've been interviewed by innumerable journalists and academics. I've been honoured to sit on panels alongside lawyers, Indigenous Elders, politicians, farmers, environmentalists, food justice and sovereignty activists, academics, and students at various levels. These have all been out-of-this-world moments for me. Nothing prepared me for all of this. I never pictured it in my mind, I never saw it coming. I had no idea of the network and organizing platform J4MW had in place.

Public speaking came with challenges too. Travelling to new places to speak to audiences full of strangers was undoubtedly nerve-racking. For the two and a half years that I was active with Justicia but still in the process of applying for permanent residency, I also lived in constant fear that the things I was saying would affect my application. This was a heavy burden.

Another challenge of my activism is the widespread ignorance, misconceptions, and myths about migrant farm labour among the Canadian general public. Some of the most common misconceptions or uninformed comments I hear are:

- "Migrant workers are taking away the good jobs."
- Speaking about farmers: "Oh, it's just a few bad apples who are the problem."
- "Migrant workers live like kings in their home countries."
- "If the conditions are so bad in Canada, then why do they keep coming back?"
- From farmers: "I treat my workers like family."
- "Everyone should just buy local!" (People who say this often don't consider that their "local" produce is grown and harvested by ultra-exploited migrant workers who are anything but local.)

Knowing the truth about these things and the desire to correct people's misconceptions is part of what pushes me to continue in my activism.

I take public speaking very seriously. I try to be an engaging public speaker, using props and humour to interact with the audience. I draw a little from both Socrates—asking my audience a lot of questions— and the iconic Sayleetar, the principal at the school where I taught (and previously attended) in La Ressource. I try to make it impossible for anybody to fall asleep during my talks. After one talk I gave in St. Catharines, Ontario, I received some strong encouragement about this goal of mine.

First, a bit of backstory. At that time, I was working on an organic farm near Kitchener. I was awaiting a decision on my permanent residency application while working alongside migrant workers from Jamaica. One of my co-workers who I became friends with was Trevor. Trevor is a very skillful worker, a busybody, and a workaholic. He works long hours performing a wide variety of jobs. With such a hectic schedule, any time that Trevor has five minutes to sit idly, it is almost certain that he will fall asleep. He became famous for this on the farm. Everyone enjoyed joking about Trevor's uncanny ability to take catnaps.

Anyway, some of my co-workers, including Trevor, attended my talk that day in St. Catharines, along with a co-owner of the farm. After my talk, the farmer said loudly, in front of everyone: "The fact that Trevor did not fall asleep during the presentation says how powerful it was." That made me laugh, but it was also a very encouraging comment.

Actually, at one of my talks at York University, a student did start falling asleep, but he approached me afterwards to apologize and explain that he had taken a medication that made him drowsy. Aside from that instance, I don't think anyone has ever fallen asleep during my talks!

Organizers and colleagues with J4MW gave me help and guidance in developing my public speaking abilities. Chris and Tzazná, the two organizers I'd met at the Hampstead vigil, as well as Tanya Ferguson, another J4MW organizer, gave me a lot of coaching and advice. I like to say that this trio cut my mouth open from one inch to one foot wide after I joined J4MW.

◇◇◇

Reactions to my presentations are almost always positive. A lot of Canadians are shocked when they hear my story. They tell me things like, "I had no idea these things are happening here." Just like me before I joined the program, they have a different idea of what Canada is and what it should be.

I've had people come up to me in tears after my presentations. I remember one university student who approached me and said,

QUESTIONS I POSE TO AUDIENCES

1. Are you concerned whether your food is being produced by those who respect or exploit the soil, the environment, and migrant workers?

2. Whose story are you familiar with: the victor's or the victim's?

3. What motivates you: a life of fear or a life of hope?

4. Which one do you prefer: a kiss or a slap? What if the kiss is a lie and the slap is the truth? What if the lie is like a painkiller, giving instant results but not a cure, and the truth is like surgery, painful at first, but which eventually heals?

5. Do you pay attention to the comforting *words* of the politicians or their actual *policies* and how they impact workers?

6. Do you pay attention to how race disconnected us, religion separated us, politics divided us, and wealth classified us?

7. Are you aware of the benevolence of Canada? When one hand gives under the flashing light of the camera, the other hand grabs in the shadow.

"Thank you for helping me understand why I chose this course of study." Others see me speak, hear me on the radio, or see me in the newspaper and offer to help me and J4MW in all sorts of ways. I see all these responses as big successes of my activism, and they encourage me to keep going.

A lot of people tell me that they love my use of props and the simplicity of my message. This is music to my ears, because I had originally been nervous about using props, thinking that in a developed country like Canada, props would be seen as archaic and that PowerPoint slides were the modern way. But I mustered the courage to use props—everything from placards to pieces of fruit to live plants—and do without PowerPoint, and the results have paid off.

Of course, not everyone likes my presentations. A very small number of times, I've had people walk out early from my talks, appearing unhappy with what I'm saying. But the number of walkouts I've had is more or less equal to the number of apologies I've received from people who feel some guilt about their ancestry: everyone from the children of farmers to the descendants of slave owners. So one compensates for the other—that's how I measure it. To me these are reminders that people are at different stages in the process of confronting the truth of what Canada actually is.

Another great thing about the presentations and appearances I've made is all the different people I've been able to connect with. Canadian society is diverse and multicultural, and I often speak in very multicultural settings. A challenge for me has been to get diverse groups to all laugh at the same time and at the same thing. When I'm able to do that, it feels like a big success.

Speaking to these different groups has also given me the opportunity to learn so much from other activists—for example, hearing from union organizers about the victories they've won and gains that they've made. That tells me that our struggle is worthwhile and that we can win. That gives me encouragement. To fight a fight that you think that you cannot win is already a losing battle. But if you know and you feel that you can win, that is victory.

I've also learned from my friends in the labour movement that all the gains and victories that unions have won were not fly-by-night accomplishments. Instead, they came as a result of careful planning. This also inspires me. We have a plan to win. We know that human-made injustices can be, will be, and must be changed. These insights have essentially become my motto and guiding principles. By and large, unions have now embraced J4MW. This is a dramatic turnaround, since previously unions had very little interest in agriculture, where it is notoriously difficult to organize. We see that we can act together and that there is strength in numbers. This is all encouraging as well.

I grew up in a top-to-bottom culture, where we expect things to come from the top and trickle down. We too often depend on someone or something magical to intervene and transform our situation. That's the culture I was raised in. Getting involved in activism has been a game changer for me, learning that bottom-up organizing yields results.

Chapter 23
SPEAKING TRUTH TO POWER

An important moment in my activism came in 2016 when I, alongside Gina Bahiwal (a Filipina former vegetable packing worker), testified before the HUMA Committee of the House of Commons as part of its review of Canada's temporary foreign worker program.[40] I did so while my application for permanent residency was still in process. My collaborator Edward Dunsworth tells me that this was probably the first time in Canadian history that migrant farm workers testified before a parliamentary committee.

The committee's review of the temporary foreign worker program (not only the SAWP, but all the various streams that bring guest workers to Canada) was the result of years of activism and media coverage about the abuses within the program. We in J4MW and our allies weren't very happy with the way the review was designed. The committee spoke to twenty witnesses representing employers and just seven temporary foreign workers, with only two of us—Gina and me—having worked in agriculture. I was the only witness who had worked in the SAWP, by far the longest-running temporary foreign worker scheme in Canada. Still, we decided to participate, and Chris Ramsaroop of J4MW and Syed Hussan of Migrant Workers Alliance for Change worked tirelessly to ensure that voices of migrant workers would be heard during the review.

Chris and Hussan (he goes by his second name) were able to secure spots for me and Gina to testify before the committee. We were only given seven minutes to speak, split between the two of us—so three and a half minutes each—something that I only learned a few minutes before my testimony. Can you imagine that?

My testimony was scheduled for May 16. I couldn't afford to take the time off work (I was working at a furniture manufacturer in Toronto at the time), so I had to deliver my comments by video call. I took the afternoon off in order to make it downtown on time for my spot in the schedule. Chris and Hussan had a computer and webcam set up at a house downtown. My taxi barely made it in time. I was so worried about being late that I didn't have time to be nervous about my testimony. In my very brief time in front of the assembled members of Parliament, I wanted to make sure that I spoke for the thousands of farm workers in the program and to make sure that our voices were heard.

Here is some of what I said:

Imagine how much harder it is when speaking up doesn't just mean losing your job, but it means being forced to leave the country. Imagine how hard it is when your employer controls your housing, and your contract is not enforceable. . . . Migrant workers are physically separated from their families and loved ones. This contributes to family breakdown of the migrant worker and a vicious cycle of poverty and social ills. Spending time with our families is more important than spending money on them. We cannot bring our families with us to Canada. . . .

Canada [is] a developed country that prides itself as a place of safe refuge. Canada prides itself as a place of diversity and inclusiveness. Canada prides itself as a place where human rights are guaranteed to all. We call on this Canada today to grant fairness to all workers. We ask Canada to grant fairness to migrant workers because we deserve the same rights as every worker in Canada. We ask Canada today to grant migrant workers their opportunity and ability to unionize and bargain collectively. We ask Canada to grant migrant farm workers open work permits. Ultimately, we ask Canada to grant migrant farm workers permanent status on arrival.

Gina's testimony was very powerful and gave the perspective of temporary foreign workers on year-round contracts, who were subject to the four-in, four-out rule that I mentioned in an earlier chapter. She talked about her struggles with securing work in Canada, having to pay multiple recruiters to find jobs, and with her immigration status after she had her application for permanent residency denied because her income was not high enough. Here are some of Gina's comments:

> The four-year rule is making us more vulnerable. Being here in Canada for four years or more, we have no life to go back to in our countries. We are separated from our families and most of us, migrant workers, have lost our families. One thing more, we don't have jobs to go back to.
>
> We came with a closed work permit and we have to stick to our employers even when they are abusive. It is hard for us to get another job or a new job because of our closed work permit. Most employers are dependent on recruiters and we pay thousands to get employment.
>
> Access to health care is a problem for migrant women and injured workers. Migrant women who get pregnant and fired from work do not have access to health care. Injured workers who are being sent home cannot access health care here in Canada.
>
> I have been talking to many migrant workers across Canada and we are shouting the same thing. It's for status upon arrival. If other migrant workers, under the skilled category, have status upon arrival, then why can't we have that too?
>
> They come here with their families. Why are we separated from our families?

Some of what both Gina and I said was included in the committee's final report.[41] But in the end, we were disappointed by the report, which made only band-aid recommendations for improving the program. Some of these were minor victories, such as a recommendation that Employment and Social Development Canada take action to ensure that migrant workers are aware of their rights. This resulted in some funding for programs doing just that with migrant farm workers. In fact, in 2021, I began a job with a program receiving this funding. At the time of writing, in August 2022, I am still in this position, although it is a short-term contract appointment.

The reason it's a short-term contract is that the funding for the overall project is very unstable, never guaranteed for more than a year at a time. This situation—the government claims credit for funding projects to assist migrant workers, while structuring that funding in a way that weakens those very efforts—gives me a lot of doubt about how much good can come from this initiative. To me, the simple question is: Will the government ever fund a genuine program that will transform this rotten, racist system that they created and maintain? Millions of dollars are spent in the name of "empowering" migrant workers, but their fundamental vulnerabilities are left untouched.

So as I said, overall the HUMA Committee's recommendations were band-aid solutions, and they did not address our fundamental demand of permanent status upon arrival. We would continue the struggle for permanent status later that same year, in my biggest activist campaign yet.

Chapter 24
THE CARAVAN

The biggest campaign I've participated in as an activist took place in 2016, my first year out of the farm worker program. To mark the fiftieth anniversary of the SAWP, J4MW organized the Harvesting Freedom Caravan, which travelled 1,500 kilometres over one month, from Leamington to Windsor to Ottawa with many stops along the way, all to demand permanent status on arrival for migrant workers. Over one thousand migrant farm workers participated in the campaign, workers from Mexico, the Caribbean, Thailand, Philippines, Indonesia, Guatemala, and Peru.

The Caravan kicked off in Leamington on the first Sunday of September, with a dinner and workshop with migrant farm workers. The following day, we joined the Labour Day parade in Windsor before heading east, making stops over the next month in Chatham, London, Tillsonburg, Simcoe, Kitchener, Cambridge, Waterloo, Hamilton, Guelph, Niagara, Toronto, Oshawa, Cobourg, and Kingston, before finally reaching Ottawa in early October.

The Harvesting Freedom campaign was a month-long whirlwind of activity for me and the other J4MW activists. It included direct action, farm visits, demonstrations, town hall meetings, public talks, meetings with allies, screenings of Min Sook Lee's excellent documentary *Migrant Dreams* (which came out the same year), fundraisers, press conferences, and endless media interviews.

Our first big direct action was at the Grande Parade of the Niagara Wine and Grape Festival in St. Catharines, Ontario. The festival is an annual celebration of Niagara's $4 billion wine industry and draws many thousands of tourists to its wineries. The Grande Parade is the highlight of the festival, featuring floats from local schools, community groups, emergency services—and of course, grape growers and wineries. Not usually featured in the parade are the migrant workers on whose backs the sector is built. We decided to change that.

Uninvited, we joined the colourful, festive parade with our banners and posters demanding status and better treatment for migrant workers who maintain the vineyards of Niagara. To the displeasure of farmers and parade organizers, we used our megaphone to shout out chants, bringing attention to the injustices, poor working and living conditions, and their remedies. They stopped the parade several times to force us out, but we were prepared and had someone assigned to negotiate. The thousands of spectators were either openly supportive or simply remained neutral by saying nothing. We marched for most of the parade, until we felt our message had been heard and our presence felt, and then we left on our own accord.

We conducted another big and strategically important action at the Ontario Food Terminal, in Toronto, the largest food distribution centre in Canada. For twenty-four hours a day, seven days a week, delivery trucks drive in and out of the terminal, depositing produce from farms and carrying it back out to grocery stores and restaurants across Canada and the United States. In other words, the terminal is a critical link in the food chain, an important stage in the process whereby the labour of migrant farm workers is converted into big profits for farmers, warehousers, shippers, and retailers.

Early on a chilly Sunday morning in late September, a group of about 150 of us gathered at the terminal. Armed with signs shaped like tomatoes and sweet peppers lettered with messages like "You're eating injustice. Status now!" we picketed at the entrance, backing up the truck traffic down the road and even up the exit ramp and onto the highway that runs right by the terminal. We chanted and heard speeches; I gave one myself. Not wanting to put any of our non-status members and friends at risk by getting arrested, after a couple of hours we pulled back from the entrance and allowed the truck traffic to resume. We continued our demonstration on the sidewalk, enjoying a pancake breakfast prepared on-site by organizers.

Another way that we took our demands up the food chain was by leafletting at farmers' markets in Chatham, London, Kitchener, and Ottawa, asking people to consider a little more deeply where their "local" produce came from. We were kicked out of all four farmers' markets. Another touchy moment happened in Cobourg. When our march blocked the street, I was confronted by a police officer who wanted us off the street. At the time, I had no immigration status, so it was an anxiety-inducing experience. Fortunately we were reaching the end of our march anyway, so the confrontation did not escalate any further.

We also showed up at the offices of various power brokers within the temporary foreign worker programs to present our demands and request meetings. We paid an unannounced visit to the Cambridge constituency office of Liberal member of Parliament Bryan May, who was chairing the HUMA Committee, where I had testified earlier that year. The committee released its report on the review of the temporary foreign worker program during the Caravan, and we wanted to voice our displeasure with its band-aid recommendations. In Guelph, we dropped in on the Ontario Federation of Agriculture and the Workplace Safety and Insurance Board, the body in charge of workers' compensation in Ontario. At most of these places, we were turned away, told that the members of Parliament or high-level staffers were not available or that our demands were unreasonable.

We met with so many workers and allies along the way, in Leamington, Chatham, Tillsonburg, Simcoe, and Cobourg. We visited farms and had cookouts with workers. We organized a health fair for migrant farm workers on a Friday afternoon in Simcoe. We held an online fundraiser for the thirty-two Jamaican farm workers whose bunkhouse had burned to ground that July, destroying all their belongings along with it, including passports. Luckily, no one was injured, but they received little support from their liaison officer, who, believe it or not, told them they would have to cover the cost of replacing their passports themselves. The opportunity to meet migrant farm workers from many countries, working all across the province, was a big highlight of the Caravan for me.

Another special moment was when we visited Six Nations of the Grand River and met with community leaders. We wanted to acknowledge that the Caravan was travelling over Indigenous lands and to seek the blessing of Six Nations to carry out our campaign on parts of their ancestral territory. The delegates we met with were supportive of the campaign and shared with us their own struggles with the Canadian government over treaty lands. We came away from the meeting with a strong sense of solidarity with our Six Nations friends.

We picketed in solidarity with striking librarians in Essex County. We participated in and addressed the Labour Day parade in Windsor. We met with many union allies across the province, such as Unifor, the Public Service Alliance of Canada (PSAC), OPSEU, and CUPE. We received encouragement from members of the New Democratic Party (NDP), both federal and provincial, and from the Green Party of Ontario and the National Farmers Union, especially Ella Haley and Richard Tunstall. We also had the unwavering support of members of the LGBTQ2S community. One act of solidarity that I remember fondly is when three white high school students joined our march in Blenheim, in Chatham County.

The Caravan ended in Ottawa, where we held a press conference at the Parliament Buildings. The next day, we held an upbeat rally in front of the Department of Immigration. At the rally were migrant farm workers from Trinidad and Tobago, Jamaica, Mexico, Philippines, and St. Lucia; supporters from Toronto, Cobourg, Ottawa, Montreal, and elsewhere; allies from Inter Pares and various unions; students, photographers, and journalists. NDP member of Parliament Niki Ashton, a great ally of migrant workers, addressed the crowd. One of the highlights of the rally was a dance performance by Juan Luis Mendoza de la Cruz and Heryka Miranda. Juan, a migrant farm worker from Mexico, had collaborated with Heryka, a choreographer, to create a dance routine based on Juan's experiences working on a sunflower farm as a migrant worker. They called the dance *The Sunflower Man*. (Sadly, Juan would pass away in Mexico in 2021 as a result of COVID-19.)

A handful of us were also permitted to enter Parliament and stand in the public gallery during a session of the House of Commons. Niki Ashton posed a question in the House: "Mr. Speaker, the temporary foreign worker program is a source of national embarrassment. Today, migrant workers, advocates, and labour brought their calls for status and justice to Ottawa. The reality is that migrant workers in Canada are exploited. Their rights are abused and they are under constant threat of deportation. We also know that the program puts downward pressure on Canadian wages. This is exploitation by design. Will the government stop the rhetoric, listen to migrant workers, and end the exploitation?"

Ashton was also instrumental in securing us a meeting with MaryAnn Mihychuk, who at the time was minister of employment, workforce development, and labour. We presented her with a petition signed by thousands of people over the course of the Caravan, demanding status for migrant workers. To me, Mihychuk was a great dancer. She danced all around the issues, shifting the conversation to tell us inane details such as how much she loved preserved fruits from Trinidad.

The Caravan was the result of months of planning, organizing, and fundraising by many J4MW activists and allies. Tzazná was the coordinator who kept tabs on things for that grand event. We set up committees in the cities and towns where our biggest profile actions would occur. In Windsor and Leamington, J4MW activist Megan Quinton collaborated with helpful people like Melisa LaRue, Elizabeth Ha, and Riam Mingmitr. In Toronto and for the Caravan in general, many, many people were instrumental in planning and executing such a huge event. Here are just a few of them: Binish Ahmed, Fatin Chowdhury, Edward Dunsworth, Evelyn Encalada Grez, Claudia Espinoza, Tanya Ferguson, Jenna Hennebry, Alia Karim, Min Sook Lee, Christine Magno, Shane Martínez, Janet McLaughlin, Elizabeth Mudenyo, Adriana Paz, Jessica Ponting, Chris Ramsaroop, Moilene Samuels, Navjeet Sidhu, Sonia Singh, Adrian Smith, Vania Tanamachi, Oriel Varga, Rathika Vasavithasan, Vasanthi Venkatesh, Alexander Vernon, Nicole Wall, and Anelyse Weiler.

For my own involvement, I had a lot of support and mentorship from Tzazná, who helped especially with public speaking, and from Chris Ramsaroop, who took care of all the invitations, made all the travel arrangements, and handled so much more. We also had an immense amount of support, including financial support, from our friend Bill Fairbairn and his Ottawa-based organization Inter Pares.

Harvesting Freedom made us look and feel powerful. The campaign was our biggest and boldest statement about who we were, and it challenged us to a new level of what was possible. Not only did it strengthen our members' unity, but also being embraced by unions for the first time was a huge success.

The Harvesting Freedom campaign was mind-blowing for me in so many ways. This was really where I discovered my role as an activist. To connect with workers all along the food chain, to connect with allies all across Ontario, to share my story and educate people everywhere from universities to churches to theatres to farmers' markets, to participate in direct actions like the one at the Food Terminal—all of that was huge to me. There were so many things that were firsts for me. Chris, Tzazná, Bill, and really J4MW and our allies as a whole created the opportunity, the stage, for me to speak and to meet with so many people. They gave me opportunities to hone the skills that I needed. The Harvesting Freedom Caravan was the mould that shaped me into the person I am today.

HARVESTING FREEDOM CARAVAN
Ottawa, October 3, 2016

Photos: Christopher Katsarov Luna

Demonstration at the offices of Immigration, Refugees and
Citizenship Canada in downtown Ottawa. Gabriel in the centre,
and holding the megaphone.

Demonstration at the offices of Immigration, Refugees and Citizenship Canada in downtown Ottawa. Holding the megaphone is Tzazná Miranda Leal.

Gabriel in downtown Ottawa (*top*) and Parliament Hill (*bottom*).

Top: Members of J4MW on Parliament Hill.
Bottom: Gabriel speaks at a press conference on Parliament Hill. Beside him are caregiver activist Christine Magno (*left*) and Tzazná Miranda Leal of J4MW (*right*).

Chapter 25

NEW BEGINNINGS AND
FUTURE HARVESTS

The best part of becoming a permanent resident for me was the euphoric feeling that came with knowing that I would be reunited with my family, that my children, Gania and Christi, would be able to join me in Canada. I think the stars were all aligned to make that possible for us. At the moment when I became a permanent resident, my son was over the age (eighteen) at which a child could be sponsored by their parent for immigration. But just one month after I gained my status, the Liberal government increased the maximum age to twenty-two. I felt like the universe had conspired in our favour. In May 2019, twenty months after I became a permanent resident, Gania and Christi finally joined me in Canada, to start a new chapter in our journey.

Of course, having my children join me in Canada brought out some new challenges. To me, they will always be my children. The shock of my life came when they told me that I was treating them as children and that they disliked it. Dealing with the fact that they were no longer actually children that I could mould was painful. The feeling that, in all the time we had spent apart, they had slipped through my fingers came rushing back in these moments. That was uncomfortable.

In the years I had been working on getting Gania and Christi to Canada, I had been looking forward to continuing the sort of life that we had together in St. Lucia. In St. Lucia, we all slept together on one bed. I was looking forward to tender moments like these. But my kids were now young adults and did not want those sorts of things. They wanted, and demanded, things on their terms. The question of whether the damages of family separation could ever be repaired was now staring me right in the eye.

My housing situation was also not what they expected. At that time, I was renting one bedroom in an apartment and sharing the kitchen and other common areas with four housemates. Making this even more complicated and challenging was the fact that when she arrived in Canada, Christi was pregnant, entering her last trimester.

It was also difficult for Gania and Christi to start new lives in an unfamiliar country, a rich nation with a totally different culture and a sometimes challenging climate. Luckily, they arrived in May, so the climate was not a shock for their first few months in Canada. And that also gave us plenty of opportunities to get out of our cramped living quarters and do things outdoors.

I am happy that their first experience of Canada was in Toronto, where I have some extremely supportive family members (like Olga, Kurt, Colette, Felona, Nadia, Lennox, and Kirby) and great friends and neighbours (like Lavina, Winter, and Pam, also known as "Pinky") that made their transition so much easier.

Fortunately, in the few years since they've arrived, Gania and Christi have adapted well, in spite of the fact that most of that time has coincided with the COVID-19 pandemic. They are both working, they've gotten comfortable getting around in Toronto (with Gania getting his licence and now driving), they've made friends, and in general they've carved out more independent lives for themselves.

As they settle into their new home in Canada, my greatest hopes for Gania and Christi are two-fold. First, that they will recognize and make use of the opportunities available here to break away from the vicious cycle of poverty and social ills that we managed to escape from in Belmont. And second, that they will discover and pursue the things that they are passionate about. It took me forty-five years to discover my passion for activism. I hope they might find their passions sooner.

◇◇◇

Recently, I embarked on another exciting new beginning. On July 17, 2021, I married my best friend, Sharna, in a simple but elegant ceremony at the picturesque Stony Hill in my home country.

I got married to someone who has been my friend for about sixteen years. For sixteen years we've been on a similar life journey but with different timing.

Two extremely strong and strange forces conspired to bring us together when we least expected it. First was the loss of my eighty-six-year-old mom in 2020, which brought me home to mourn. And second was the COVID-19 pandemic, which caused Sharna to be laid off from her tourism job, but also gave us the opportunity to reconnect during my time at home.

I had always wished to have friendship as a strong base for my marriage. My marriage to Sharna has taken me to a stage and level that I have never been to, but that my past has prepared me for. We are now eagerly awaiting a response for our sponsorship application to bring Sharna to Canada and begin a new chapter together.

◇◇◇

Having been denied so much and for so long, I am determined to reap all the harvests that come with having status in Canada. I want to make up for all the difficulties I faced while living in constant fear during my time as a migrant farm worker.

It feels so good to be on the verge of a new, fuller life. I thank my past for preparing me for this beautiful milestone. Living life with hope, knowing that my tomorrow will be better than my today is one of my biggest and best natural medicines. I look forward to all the beautiful things life has to offer in abundance, living with the ones I love and who love me.

◇◇◇

It has been a long and bumpy road full of uncertainties to get to the point where I am now, living permanently in Canada, reunited with my children, newly married, a homeowner, and pursuing my activist work. As I think about the road I've travelled and look forward to the road ahead, I have many hopes for the future of the struggle for justice for migrant workers.

My biggest hope, of course, is that we will be victorious in winning permanent status for all workers upon arrival in Canada. To get there will involve many steps along the way, and those victories will need to be part of a bigger set of changes.

Along the way to that ultimate goal, I hope that many more Canadians will come to know the injustices that migrant workers face in Canada. That more will become aware of and concerned about how their food is being produced. That they will fight for a Canadian food system that is healthy, sustainable, and just, by demanding that their food be produced by those who respect the soil, the environment, and migrant workers.

I also hope that migrant justice and food justice will become part of the curriculum at all levels and will be taught in ways that make learning fun. And that students will understand the historical context of slavery, colonialism, capitalism, and global inequality that shapes these issues.

I am hoping that this book will be read far and wide and help raise awareness about the conditions of migrant workers, and that this awareness will inspire the public to pressure politicians to change the unjust laws and policies that oppress migrant workers. I hope that, for people who see temporary foreign workers as taking Canadian jobs or lowering Canadian wages, this book might encourage them to see migrant workers instead as *fellow* workers, as allies in a bigger fight for a society in which everyone benefits from social and economic inclusion.

I hope, too, that this book will be read by many migrant workers, from many countries. I hope that it will empower and instill some hope in migrant workers and push them to share their own stories and take action to create a more just Canadian food system.

As we work towards a healthy, sustainable, and just food system, I hope that migrant farm workers in Ontario—and across Canada— will soon be unionized.

For my group, J4MW, I hope that in the near future we will have a larger pool of volunteers, with diverse skills. I hope that we can one day have an office as our base of operations. I hope, too, that we can continue to discover new strategies to enlighten and empower migrant workers to overcome fear, share their stories and experiences, and join our movement.

I hope that we will work more closely with our allies, including both the NDP and the Green Party of Canada, and get more federal and provincial legislators elected to bring about the policy changes we need. I hope that we can continue to build alliances with Indigenous peoples and link our struggles for justice, dignity, and freedom together.

Knowing that our extremely difficult working and living conditions in Canada are the result of unjust policies crafted by politicians in collaboration with business interests, I feel extremely confident that meaningful and lasting change in Canada is possible. The fact that more Canadians are concerned about where and how their foods are being produced—something that we saw even more as a result of the Harvesting Freedom campaign and especially during the COVID-19 pandemic—makes me confident that lasting change is not just possible, but that it will become a reality.

◇◇◇

My first grandchild, Lorenzo Star Allahdua, was born on August 28, 2019. He is healthy, active, playful, friendly, and smart. He is a bundle of joy to all those who are in touch with him.

Lorenzo is now the third generation of Allahduas in Canada, with Gania and Christi, Lorenzo's mom, being the second generation. It is my hope that Lorenzo will not face all the hardships that I faced as a first-generation migrant—and later immigrant—in Canada. It is also my wish that he will recognize and take advantage of all the opportunities that are available to him in this land and live life to his fullest potential.

Ultimately, I hope that Lorenzo will live to see the end of dehumanizing and exploitative migrant labour programs in Canada, and that he will enjoy the harvests of all the fruits that we migrant workers and immigrants have sown as part of our fight to make Canada a more just and equitable society.

I AM MANY THINGS
(reprise)

I am many things in Canada . . .

a God
reclaiming my dignity,
my godly position
that was snatched from me

an Angel
with a message of justice for the world

a Slave
proud of my ancestry
fighting to break the chains that held my forebears
and that still hold their descendants today

a Half Human
who has found his other half

a Lab Rat
who has escaped from the maze

and has come back to show others the way out.

COVID-19 AND MIGRANT
FARM WORKERS

Gabriel Allahdua & Edward Dunsworth
in Conversation

I n March 2020, as the COVID-19 pandemic took hold in Canada, one of the earliest responses of the federal government was to sharply curtail the arrival of travellers from abroad. With the exception of US citizens and certain workers, all foreigners were forbidden from entering Canada. This included migrant farm workers. Predictably, the growers' lobby rose quickly up in arms, warning of labour shortages and of crops left to rot in fields. Within four days, the government reversed course and decided to grant entry to migrant farm workers, with the requirement that workers quarantine for fourteen days upon arrival.

Despite warnings from advocates, however, authorities gave little thought to the safety of workers once their quarantines had elapsed. To the surprise of no one who had been paying attention, the crowded bunkhouses where temporary foreign labourers live proved to be the perfect environment for the spread of the virus. Thousands of migrant farm workers contracted COVID in the first year of the pandemic, before the roll-out of vaccines could offer some protection. In Ontario in 2020, migrant farm workers were ten times more likely to get COVID than a member of the general public. In that first year, three migrant farm workers, all from Mexico, died as a result of the virus. Despite the protection afforded by vaccination, 2021 proved to be an even deadlier year for migrant farm workers, with at least nine dying in Canada, six during the two-week quarantine. Only one of those deaths has been publicly confirmed to have been the result of COVID-19, but the rate of death in 2021 was more than four times higher than that of a typical year for the SAWP.

Throughout the pandemic, migrant justice activists like Gabriel and his colleagues in Justicia for Migrant Workers have sounded the alarm about workers' conditions and continued to beat the drum for permanent status upon arrival. Despite platitudes from politicians, their demands have not yet been heeded, despite the massive sacrifices made by these "front-line workers" in maintaining Canada's food supply during the pandemic. On January 21, 2022, I sat down with Gabriel for a conversation about migrant farm workers' experiences of the pandemic. A transcript from that conversation was published in the March 2022 edition of *Syndemic Magazine* and is partially reprinted here, lightly edited, with the kind permission of its editor, Ian McKay.

ED: What has been the experience of migrant farm workers during the COVID-19 pandemic? Has the pandemic worsened conditions for migrant farmworkers, or has it simply exposed pre-existing problems?

GA: The pandemic has both exposed and worsened the situation. It has exposed Canada's dirty secret. Up until recently, vulnerable migrant workers have been invisible, but the pandemic has forced mainstream media to place the camera on them. In fact, what it has taken activists twenty years to do, the pandemic has exposed in a couple of months.

During the pandemic, the borders were closed and for a time open only to permanent residents and citizens. But it didn't take long for the prime minister to open borders for migrant workers. Migrant workers are treated differently at the border now. They run through customs. They're now considered essential workers. *Essential.* That's a transformation. But, aside from speeding up their entry into Canada, migrant farm workers were not treated like essential workers. They never got hazard pay. They were not treated like other front-line workers.

Migrant workers' living and working conditions are both isolated and overcrowded. It is a recipe for COVID-19 to spread like wildfire. Many, many migrant farm workers have gotten sick, and some have died.[42]

In mid-January 2022, the Windsor-Essex County Health Unit put a stop to migrant workers entering the county. Why? Because there were so many migrant workers in quarantine that there was no more space for them. That highlights the dire living and working conditions faced by migrant workers.

ED: Can you tell us a bit about how migrant farm workers' housing conditions helped facilitate the spread of COVID-19?

GA: In the bunkhouse where I lived, there were typically eight workers per room. Newly constructed bunkhouses typically have up to fourteen people per room. The kitchens are communal, and bathrooms are shared. None of this complies with social distancing protocol, which made it very easy for COVID-19 to spread among workers. The program is focused on profit and not on the health or welfare of workers.

ED: What has been the response of various levels of government to the pandemic as it affects migrant farm workers? What does this tell us about the value placed on migrant workers' lives?

GA: The response has been varied. Let me start with housing. In Norfolk County, the chief medical officer wanted to have three workers per bunkhouse. The farmers pushed back because they thought it was an inefficient use of bunkhouses. Municipal governments have not done much and have always acted in favour of the employers. Ontario has never provided us with the hazard pay that it provided to other front-line workers. That shows that migrant farm workers are in a different class. Every level of government has been giving lip service, but not taking action. The fact that the federal government opened the border for migrant farm workers highlights how important migrant workers are to the economy. With high unemployment, I thought Canadians would work on the farms. But Canadians still do not want to do that work, because the conditions are neither attractive nor just. The federal government's policies are geared towards putting food on Canadians' tables, not creating the conditions that are attractive for workers. They do things that favour the profits of employers and not the well-being of workers.

ED: How has COVID-19 affected St. Lucia? What have been the ramifications for St. Lucian migrant workers?

GA: St. Lucia depends heavily on tourism, which COVID-19 has affected significantly. The main sources of tourists to St. Lucia—the United Kingdom, Canada, and the United States—all banned flights early in the pandemic. Hotel workers and taxi drivers were laid off as a result. Because of that, unemployed people could not pay their loans. Less income per household meant less money available for food, utilities, and so on. Mass unemployment around the world has also affected our exports. COVID security measures, such as tests and quarantine, have both affected workers' ability to travel and put them at risk of infection. The lack of flights meant that many had to rely on more expensive charter flights to travel. Most worryingly, the government of Jamaica required workers to sign a waiver declaring that they were travelling to Canada at their own risk. So, many workers decided not to travel, because they were not sure where they stood or what support they would receive from their own governments.

ED: What has been the experience of migrant workers during their two-week quarantines after they arrive in Canada?

GA: The common issues that they face revolve around food. Some farmers do provide quarantined workers with adequate food. But in many cases workers either aren't given enough food, or they are provided with food that is culturally inappropriate. In one case, the only bread provided to workers for their fourteen-day quarantine was a single loaf, and the only meat provided was a single whole chicken. To top it off, the workers were charged exorbitant prices for this insufficient amount of food. Workers at hotels or government facilities also complained about the food. They send me pictures of the breakfast given to them: a banana and a yogurt. That is not a West Indian breakfast. Other companies did not allow people to bring food to quarantined people. Another issue was pay, specifically quarantine pay. Workers were quarantined because there was an outbreak at work, or in their homes, or in their bunkhouses. It was not clear who would pay them and how much they would get paid.

ED: Do you want to say anything about the migrant workers who have died of COVID?

GA: When workers come to Canada, not only are they risking their health, but they're also risking their lives. The high number of infected workers shows that they are always in danger. Quite a few of the

workers have died in suspicious circumstances and the cause of death has not always been confirmed. As with many issues surrounding migrant workers, we are left in the dark.

ED: Yeah, there were a very unusual number of workers who died during their quarantine. Especially since in Ontario, migrant farm workers were ten times as likely as the general population to contract COVID-19. That's a really staggering statistic that speaks to how much the living and working conditions contributed to the spread of the disease.

GA: Exactly, and to top it all off the government has been relaxing requirements and making it easier for farmers to bring in workers.

ED: Can you tell me a bit about the work that you've done with migrant workers during the pandemic, both as an activist and as a staff member with a service-providing agency?

GA: Let me start with the Trinidadians. In 2021, the borders in Trinidad were closed. This meant that, as winter approached, many Trinidadians couldn't return home after they completed their seasons picking ginseng, apples, and tobacco. Because their work permits had ended, they were not entitled to employment insurance. They were also not equipped to spend the winter in Canada. I worked with them to provide the clothes, food, and other supplies they needed to make it through the winter comfortably. My group, Justice for Migrant Workers, also pressured the government to get these workers an open work permit so they were not stranded in Canada without legal status.

I also worked with a group of over twenty Barbadians in the Blue Mountain area. They were not farm workers, but instead were working in tourism. After the hotel closed due to COVID-19, they had no more wages coming in and were not receiving employment insurance. They were moved to smaller, cramped accommodations with malfunctioning heating. Despite these extraordinary circumstances, their employer was still charging the workers rent: over $100 a week, the same as they had been paying at their original lodging. I provided them with the same sorts of winter supplies as the Trinidadians.

I also received calls from workers (especially Jamaicans) who were either forbidden—or strongly discouraged—from leaving the farm property. This outrageous overreach of employer control meant that workers had difficulty sending money home, or buying necessary items (such as rubber boots). They also could not get culturally appropriate food. In a few cases, we were able to provide some of these items, but often we could not get onto the farm because of the strict oversight by employers.

I have also been working with TNO (The Neighbourhood Organization) as an outreach worker to get personal protective equipment (PPE) to migrant workers, helping workers to keep themselves safe. TNO is funded by the government through KAIROS. I have also been running workshops to educate workers on their rights in Canada, distributing materials from ESDC (Employment and Social Development Canada) on health and safety, who they could call if they weren't paid properly, and if they needed help more generally.

Acknowledgements

A number of people helped bring this book to fruition.

First off, we owe a huge debt of gratitude to Megan Coulter, who as a research assistant spent dozens upon dozens of hours labouring over interview transcripts and helping out in numerous other ways. Michele A. Johnson and Craig Heron provided valuable advice and support at the outset of project. Christopher Katsarov Luna gave us permission to reprint his stunning photographs from the 2016 Harvesting Freedom Caravan. Anelyse Weiler chipped in with tips and contacts. Nate Wessel made the first-rate maps. Eric MacPherson helped transcribe the epilogue interview. Historian of St. Lucia Jolien Harmsen was generous with her time and advice. Tilman Lewis was a simply outstanding editor. Between the Lines managing editor Amanda Crocker supported this project enthusiastically from the beginning, and Devin Clancy and the rest of the Between the Lines team were incredibly helpful along the way. Our sincere gratitude to all.

Ed: Thanks first and foremost to Gabriel for embarking on this project with me, for opening up your life to create this book. With a project like this, so many things could have gone wrong. None of them did. Your wisdom, patience, diligence, and understanding are an inspiration; it has been an enormous honour to work with you.

I would also like to thank my wife, Vanessa, for her support throughout this project, and my children, Ignacio and Lucía—Iggy arrived near the start of the project and Lulu at the end—for many welcome distractions.

Gabriel: This book would not have been possible without my collaborator Ed Dunsworth. Ed, I am so appreciative of your vision (you saw something I did not see, from our first encounter in 2016); your patience and persistence, dedicating so much time to bring this project to completion; your ability to draw out details that made this story a complete product; and your tireless heavy lifting on all parts of the project.

Sincere thanks as well to my friends and colleagues at Justicia for Migrant Workers. Special appreciation to The Neighbourhood Organization and manager Jennifer Rajasekar for providing a supportive environment and flexible schedule, which helped make the writing of this book possible. And heartfelt thanks to Philma Charlery, Veronica Eastman, Francis Mahon, Stephanie Mayell, Muguelle Ramanich, Althea St. Cyr, and Rania Younis for their great support.

My deepest gratitude goes to my wife, Sharna, my children, Gania and Christi, my grandson, Lorenzo, and my extended family in St. Lucia for their love and support.

NOTES

1   Jolien Harmsen, Guy Ellis, and Robert Devaux, *A History of St. Lucia* (Vieux Fort, St. Lucia: Lighthouse Road, 2014); Anderson Reynolds, *The Struggle for Survival: An Historical, Political, and Socioeconomic Perspective of St. Lucia*, 3rd ed. (New York: Jako Books, 2018); Scott M. Fitzpatrick and William F. Keegan, "Human Impacts and Adaptations in the Caribbean Islands: An Historical Ecology Approach," *Earth and Environmental Science Transactions of The Royal Society of Edinburgh* 98, no. 1 (2007): 29–45; B. W. Higman, *A Concise History of the Caribbean* (New York: Cambridge University Press, 2011), 15; Franklin W. Knight, *The Caribbean, the Genesis of a Fragmented Nationalism*, 3rd ed. (New York: Oxford University Press, 2012), 35–36, 54, 83, 132.

2   Joy Parr, "Hired Men: Ontario Agricultural Wage Labour in Historical Perspective," *Labour / Le Travail* 15 (Spring 1985): 92; Vic Satzewich, *Racism and the Incorporation of Foreign Labour: Farm Labour Migration to Canada since 1945* (New York: Routledge, 1991), 111; Clare Glassco, "Harvesting Power and Subjugation: Canada's Seasonal Agricultural Workers Program in Historical Context" (MA thesis, Trent University, 2012), 126–27; "Protection of Migrant Agricultural Workers in Canada, Mexico and the United States" (Washington, DC: Secretariat of the Commission for Labor Cooperation, 2002).

3   Edward Dunsworth, *Harvesting Labour: Tobacco and the Global Making of Canada's Agricultural Workforce* (Montreal: McGill-Queen's University Press, 2022); Robert Falconer, "Family Farmers to Foreign Fieldhands: Consolidation of Canadian Agriculture and the Temporary Foreign Worker Program," *School of Public Policy Publications* 13 (2020), doi: 10.11575/SPPP.V13I0.70741.

4   R. M. Mackie to Black, January 20, 1967, Department of Manpower and Immigration, RG118, acc. 1985-86/071, vol. 82, file 3315-5-3, part 1, Library and Archives Canada.

5   John Carr Munro, "Immigration—Temporary Harvest Workers Remaining in Canada," October 20, 1966, *Hansard Parliamentary Debates*, retrieved from LiPaD: The Linked Parliamentary Data Project, lipad.ca.

6   Satzewich, *Racism and the Incorporation of Foreign Labour*.

7   "School Opening Upsets Part-Time Work on Farms," *Toronto Star*, September 5, 1967.

8   Immigration, Refugees and Citizenship Canada, "How the Provincial Nominee Program (PNP) Works," Government of Canada, October 19, 2022, canada.ca.

9   "How Temporary Were Canada's Temporary Foreign Workers?," Statistics Canada, January 29, 2018, www150.statcan.gc.ca.

10   Jenna Hennebry, "Permanently Temporary?: Agricultural Migrant Workers and Their Integration in Canada," *IRPP Study* no. 26 (February 2012).

11   Makeda Silvera, *Silenced: Talks with Working Class West Indian Women about Their Lives and Struggles as Domestic Workers in Canada* (Toronto: Sister Vision Press, 1989 [1983]).

12   Antonio Gramsci, *Selections from the Prison Notebooks*, ed. and trans. Quintin Hoare and Geoffrey Nowell Smith (London: Lawrence and Wishart, 1971), 5.

13   Cindy Hahamovitch, *No Man's Land: Jamaican Guestworkers in America and the Global History of Deportable Labor* (Princeton: Princeton University Press, 2011), 8.

14   Satzewich, *Racism and the Incorporation of Foreign Labour*, 114; B. Celovsky, "Seasonal Agricultural and Food Processing Workers from the West Indies," February 21, 1967, Department of Manpower and Immigration, RG118, acc. 1985-86/071, vol. 81, file 3315-5-1, part 2, Library and Archives Canada.

15   Dunsworth, *Harvesting Labour*, 200–201.

16   On important wildcat strikes by Mexican greenhouse workers in Leamington, Ontario, in 2001 and 2003, see: Ofelia Becerril, "Transnational Work and the Gendered Politics of Labour: A Study of Male and Female Mexican Migrant Farm Workers in Canada," in *Organizing the Transnational: Labour, Politics, and Social Change*, ed. Luin Goldring and Sailaja Krishnamurti (Vancouver: UBC Press, 2007), 157–72. For more examples of West Indian worker protest, see: Edward Dunsworth, "'Me a

Free Man': Resistance and Racialisation in the Canada-Caribbean Seasonal Agricultural Workers Program," *Oral History* 49, no. 1 (Spring 2021): 71–82. Both these texts also discuss retributional repatriation.

17 Silvera, *Silenced*; Abigail Bess Bakan and Daiva K. Stasiulis, *Not One of the Family: Foreign Domestic Workers in Canada* (University of Toronto Press, 1997); Daiva K. Stasiulis and Abigail B. Bakan, *Negotiating Citizenship: Migrant Women in Canada and the Global System* (Toronto: University of Toronto Press, 2005).

18 Adriana Paz Ramirez, "Embodying and Resisting Labour Apartheid: Racism and Mexican Farm Workers in Canada's Seasonal Agricultural Workers Program" (MA thesis, University of British Columbia, 2013).

19 "Justicia Hampstead with Dedication," YouTube video, February 5, 2013, youtu.be/xiWGu4Rx-sE.

20 Henry Fountain, "Climate Change Is Making Hurricanes Stronger, Researchers Find," *New York Times*, May 18, 2020, nytimes.com.

21 A recent report by the National Farmers Union about addressing the twin crises of climate and agriculture, for example, notes the imperative to transition to more organic farming—a move that would dramatically increase agriculture's labour requirements. *Tackling the Farm Crisis and the Climate Crisis: A Transformative Strategy for Canadian Farms and Food Systems* (National Farmers Union, November 2019), nfu.ca.

22 The same is more or less true in the other former British colonies of the Caribbean, which are often grouped together as the West Indies or the Commonwealth Caribbean. To this day, these countries have strong links—cultural, economic, diplomatic—and St. Lucia is an active participant in international Caribbean organizations such as the Caribbean Community (CARICOM) and the Organization of Eastern Caribbean States.

23 For more on the fascinating history of the flower festivals, see Harmsen, Ellis, and Devaux, *A History of St. Lucia*, 183–87.

24 From the mid-1960s to mid-1970s, CIDA spent approximately $150 million in the Commonwealth Caribbean, building schools and infrastructure, funding a development bank, and supporting agricultural initiatives. About $1 million of those funds went towards building CCSS. Taking place in the context of the Cold War and decolonization, as more and more countries in the "developing" world were gaining independence, Canadian foreign aid was very much part of the charm offensive of rich Western nations that was aimed at bringing decolonizing countries onto their side of the Iron Curtain. Guest

worker arrangements like the SAWP were also wrapped up in this geopolitical context. "Canadian Financial Aid Big Factor in Caribbean," *Globe and Mail*, January 24, 1975; Mavis E. Burke, "An Analysis of Canadian Educational Assistance to the Commonwealth Caribbean Leeward and Windward Islands, 1960–1970" (PhD diss, University of Ottawa, 1975), 243, 317.

25   The sugar industry had struggled since the late nineteenth century, when the rise of European beet sugar (cheaper to produce and subsidized by European governments) coincided with changes in British trade policy, causing a sharp decline in the price of sugar. Though sugar survived—and remained St. Lucia's top crop—well into the twentieth century, the economic challenges only grew over time. St. Lucian farmers tried other crops over the years, including bananas, with mixed results. The decisive shift came in the 1950s when British-Dutch agricultural and shipping magnate John van Geest struck a bold marketing arrangement with banana producers on four of the Windward Islands, including St. Lucia, pledging to buy every banana produced on the islands. The arrangement proved highly attractive to both large estates and peasant producers. Banana production soared tenfold between 1954 and 1960. By 1963, sugar had disappeared altogether as a commercial crop, with bananas taking its place as the island's top export product. Harmsen, Ellis, and Devaux, *A History of St. Lucia*, ch. 11, 14; Reynolds, *Struggle for Survival*, ch. 13; Higman, *A Concise History of the Carribean*, 324; Frank J. McDonald, "St. Lucia: Bananas, Politics and Poverty," newsletter, Institute of Current World Affairs, March 20, 1969, icwa.org.

26   For more on the dam collapse, see: Camille Gaskin-Reyes, "Guyana: Collapse of the Omami [*sic*] Mine Waste Dam," *Brazil's Rio Doce Disaster*, Georgetown University, n.d., blogs.commons.georgetown.edu.

27   Varroa mite wreaked havoc on St. Lucian apiculture. Before the mite entered St. Lucia, in 1998, there were approximately 150 beekeepers on the island, managing 3,200 hives. By 2003, those numbers had been cut in half: only about 70 beekeepers and 1,500 hives remained. Dennis van Engelsdorp, "Assessment of the Apiculture Industry in St. Lucia, West Indies," Farmer to Farmer Consultation Report, March 25–April 5, 2003, apiservices.biz.

28   The United States brought a free trade complaint to the WTO, aiming to secure greater European market access for bananas produced by US-owned mega-operations in Central and South America. The WTO ultimately ruled in the United States' favour. The 1997 WTO ruling devastated banana sectors throughout the Caribbean, which could not compete with the enormous, heavily mechanized operations of mainland Latin America. St. Lucia was no exception. The 2003 banana crop, for example, was only a quarter the size of the 1990 crop. Between 1994 and 2000, St. Lucia lost an

estimated 27,000–31,000 jobs in the banana sector, a staggering number in a country with a population of just over 150,000 at the time. Harmsen, Ellis, and Devaux, *A History of St. Lucia*, 356.

29   For an excellent film about the harm caused to countries in the Global South—and Commonwealth Caribbean in particular—by international financial organizations and their policies, see *Life and Debt*, dir. Stephanie Black, 2001.

30   "Total Number of Visitor Arrivals by Type 1992 to 2020," Central Statistical Office of Saint Lucia, stats.gov.lc.

31   "Industries and Jobs with Exemptions or Special Rules: Agriculture, Growing, Breeding, Keeping and Fishing," Government of Ontario, ontario.ca.

32   Leah F. Vosko, "Blacklisting as a Modality of Deportability: Mexico's Response to Circular Migrant Agricultural Workers' Pursuit of Collective Bargaining Rights in British Columbia, Canada," *Journal of Ethnic and Migration Studies* 42, no. 8 (2016): 1371–87.

33   Serena Marotta, "'Humiliated': At Hearing, Migrant Worker Recalls OPP's DNA Sweep," *London Free Press*, November 22, 2021, lfpress.com.

34   Nicholas Keung, "Human Rights Tribunal Fines Farm $23,500 for Calling Migrant Workers 'Monkeys,'" *Toronto Star*, July 29, 2013, thestar.com.

35   "Leamington Mayor Wants 'Lewd' Jamaican Behaviour to End," *CBC News*, August 30, 2013, cbc.ca.

36   Rob Hornberger, "Increased Affordable Housing, Core Residential Development Eyed in Official Plan Revisions," *Kingsville Observer*, December 15, 2020, kingsvilleobserver.com.

37   "Desmond Tutu," in *Oxford Essential Quotations*, ed. Susan Ratcliffe, oxfordreference.com; Elie Wiesel, "Nobel Acceptance Speech," Elie Wiesel Foundation for Humanity, December 10, 1986, eliewieselfoundation.org.

38   David Werner and Bill Bower, *Helping Health Workers Learn: A Book of Methods, Aids and Ideas for Instructors at the Village Level* (Palo Alto, CA: Hesperian Foundation, 1982), 12. Book available online at healthwrights.org.

39   If you would like to see one of Gabriel's recorded talks, we especially recommend the presentation he gave at the Toronto Workers' History Project in 2017, which can be found on YouTube: youtu.be/7BoZjZyoRks.

40 The committee's full name is the Standing Committee on Human Resources, Skills and Social Development and the Status of Persons with Disabilities.

41 The proceedings and final report of the HUMA Committee's review of the temporary foreign worker program can be found on the House of Commons website: ourcommons.ca.

42 On deaths and illnesses among migrant workers during the pandemic, see, for example: Edward Dunsworth, "Insecurity via Exclusion: Migrant Farm Workers in the Age of COVID-19," ActiveHistory.ca, June 30, 2021, activehistory.ca.

INDEX

Programme for Animal Health Assistants (REPAHA), 35

Ha, Elizabeth, 151
Hahamovitch, Cindy, xvii
Haitian Revolution, 119
Haley, Ella, 150
Hampstead (Ontario), 2012 accident in, xviii, 116, 119; vigil for, 116–17, 137, 140
harassment, 125; police, 112-13, 126; sexual, 114
Harper, Stephen, 132
Harvesting Freedom campaign, xviii–xix, 161
Harvesting Freedom Caravan, 147–52, 153–56
Hay, Louise, 109
Hayes-Moise, Lena, 90–91
Hennebry, Jenna, 151
Hoyte, Desmond, 34
HUMA Committee (House of Commons), 143–46, 149
human rights, 5, 102, 125-26, 128, 129
hurricane Allen, 49
hurricane Tomas, xii, xx, 49–52; economic effects of, 53–54, 131
Hussan, Syed, 143–44

Ian (from Leamington Gospel Hall), 107
illiteracy: in Guyana, 33; in St. Lucia, 30, 31, 101–3
immigration: to Canada, xiii–xiv; from Europe, 138; and family reunification, xix; laws, 128, 137; legal status, 69, 113; permanent, xiv, 75, 126, 128, 130, 137; and rights, 138
imperialism: history of, xvii
inclusivity, 129
indenture: history of, xvii, 28
Indigenous peoples, xi–xii, 11, 160; mistreatment and oppression of, 119
Indonesia, 147

Industrial Workers of the World (IWW), 115
inequality, 40; global, 160
International Convention on the Protection of the Rights of All Migrant Workers and Members of Their Families, 129
International Monetary Fund, 38
international relations, history of, xvii
internet, 85, 94, 132
Inter Pares, 134, 150, 151
Isaac, Desmond, 35

Jamaica, xiii, xvii, 32, 74, 79, 87, 114, 117, 149, 150, 168, 169
Jones, George, 15
Justicia (Justice) for Migrant Workers (J4MW), xviii, 15, 85, 115, 116, 118, 121, 129–30, 134, 137–42, 143, 147, 151, 152, 156, 160, 166, 169

KAIROS, 170
Kalinago people, xi
Karim, Alia, 151
Kingsville (Ontario), 114

"labour apartheid," xviii
labour laws, 128, 137
labour mobility, xiii; racialized, xvii
labour standards, 126–28
labour stoppage, xviii
La Ressource, 11; Cooperative Credit Union, 40; Primary School, 22–23, 28, 29–30, 31, 139–40; Roman Catholic Combined School, 12
LaRue, Melissa, 151
Leamington (Ontario), 138, 147; anti-loitering bylaw in, 113–15; Business Improvement Area (BIA), 113; Gabriel's arrival in, 4; Gospel Hall, 106–8; as greenhouse capital of Canada, 62, 114; racism and discrimination in, 111–15; as tomato capital of Canada, 114, 115

Munro, John, xiii–xiv

National Farmers Union, 136, 150, 175n21

New Democratic Party (NDP), 150, 160

Niagara Wine and Grape Festival: Grande Parade, 147–48

Nicaragua, 116

Norfolk County, 167

Olice, Bachus, 40

Omai gold-mining corporation, 36

Ontario: agricultural employment law in, 66; Department of Agriculture and Food, xiv; *Employment Standards Act*, 127; farmers in, xiii; Human Rights Tribunal, 112–13; immigration to, xiv; *Labour Relations Act*, 129; Workplace Safety and Insurance Board, 149

Ontario Federation of Agriculture, 149

Ontario Food Terminal, 148, 152

Ontario Provincial Police (OPP), 112–13

Ontario Public Service Employees Union (OPSEU), 115, 150

Ontario Secondary School Teachers' Federation (OSSTF), 115

oppression, xvii, 90; of African Americans, 90–91; of Indigenous peoples, 119; of migrant workers, 113-14, 125, 160; structural, xviii

oral history, xix–xx

organic farming, 175n21

Organization of Eastern Caribbean States, 4, 175n22

overtime pay, 66–67, 76, 127

Paterson, John, 114

Paz, Adriana, 151

Peace Corps, 40, 134

permanent residency, xiv-xv, 15, 131–38, 143, 145, 157; for Gabriel, 15, 131–36, 139-40, 143, 157; on

humanitarian and compassionate grounds (H&C), 133

Peru, 116, 118, 147

pesticides, 19–20, 37, 77

Philippines, 147, 150

phone cards, 88, 93, 94

Point Pelee National Park, 95

"points system," xiv

police harassment, 112–13, 126

Ponting, Jessica, 151

poverty: in St. Lucia, 18–19, 22, 30, 31, 40, 95, 158

power: of employers, xiv-xv, 69-71, 93, 125, 130; literacy and, 101-3

precariousness, 103, 125, 128, 137–38

Protestantism, 12

Provincial Nominee Program, xiv

public holiday pay, 67

Public Service Alliance of Canada (PSAC), 150

Quinton, Megan, 151

racial injustice, 126

racism, xiv, 90, 111–15, 119, 126

Rampal, Michael ("Isaac"), 40

Ramsaroop, Chris, 118–19, 140, 143–44, 151, 152

residential schools, 119

Rodney, Walter, 34

Roy (gift recipient), 98

Samuels, Moilene, 151

Sandiford, Daniel ("Tarbac"), 40

Sandiford, Lucas ("Lulu"), 40

Santos, Nelson, 114

Satzewich, Vic, xiv

schistosomiasis. *See* bilharzia

Schroeter, Steven, 134

Seasonal Agricultural Worker Program (SAWP), xi, xii–xvi, xviii, xx, 5–6, 25, 32, 52, 54, 96–100, 121, 143; death rate in, 165; as employer-driven program, 129; employer power in, xiv-xv, 69-71,